CAMBRIDGE MUSIC HANDBOOKS

Monteverdi: Vespers (1610)

CAMBRIDGE MUSIC HANDBOOKS

GENERAL EDITOR Julian Rushton

Cambridge Music Handbooks provide accessible introductions to major musical works.

Monteverdi

Vespers (1610)

John Whenham

CAMBRIDGE
UNIVERSITY PRESS

PUBLISHED BY THE PRESS SYNDICATE OF THE UNIVERSITY OF CAMBRIDGE
The Pitt Building, Trumpington Street, Cambridge CB2 1RP, United Kingdom

CAMBRIDGE UNIVERSITY PRESS
The Edinburgh Building, Cambridge CB2 2RU, United Kingdom
40 West 20th Street, New York, NY 10011–4211, USA
10 Stamford Road, Oakleigh, Melbourne 3166, Australia

First published 1997

Printed in the United Kingdom at the University Press, Cambridge

Typeset in Monotype Ehrhardt 10.5/13 pt

A catalogue record for this book is available from the British Library

Library of Congress cataloguing in publication data
Whenham, John.
Monteverdi, Vespers (1610) / John Whenham.
p. cm. – (Cambridge music handbooks)
Discography: p. 134
Includes bibliographical references (p. 130) and index.
ISBN 0 521 45377 1 (hardback). – ISBN 0 521 45979 6 (paperback).
1. Monteverdi, Claudio, 1567–1643. Vespro della Beata Vergine.
I. Title. II. Series.
ML410.M77W44 1997
782.32'4–dc21 96–47886 CIP MN

ISBN 0 521 45377 1 hardback
ISBN 0 521 45979 6 paperback

AH

Contents

Contents

Acknowledgements

The preparation of a book necessarily incurs many debts of gratitude, and for their advice and help in resolving questions of various kinds I should like to thank Gregory Barnett, Laura Davey, John Edwards, John and Sally Harper, Mary O'Neill, David Parker, Valerie Edden and Duncan Fielden. Julian Rushton and Graham Dixon read earlier drafts of the book and made many helpful suggestions and criticisms for which I am most grateful. For their constant patience and support I have to thank Jenny, Nicholas and Christopher, to whom this book is dedicated.

The English translations of Latin liturgical texts quoted in Appendixes 1 and 2 are from Dom Gaspar Lefebvre, *Saint Andrew Daily Missal, with Vespers for Sunday and Feasts* (Bruges, 1954) and are used with permission.

Abbreviations

A	Alto/Altus
AM	*Antiphonale Monasticum*
B	Bass/Bassus
Bar	Baritone
BCP	The Book of Common Prayer
Bg	*Bassus generalis*
Bt	Monteverdi, *Vespers* (1610), ed. Clifford Bartlett, revised edn, Autumn 1990 (King's Music, Redcroft, Banks End, Wyton, Huntingdon, Cambridgeshire PE17 2AA, England)
C	Cantus
Ct	Counter-tenor
GB–Bu	Great Britain, Birmingham University Library
GB–Lbl	Great Britain, London, British Library
LU	*Liber Usualis*
MS(S)	Manuscript(s)
Ms	Mezzo-soprano
Q	Quintus
R	Monteverdi, *Vespro della Beata Vergine*, ed. Jerome Roche (London &c.: Eulenburg, 1994)
S	Sextus
Sop	Soprano
St	Monteverdi, *Vespers for Soloists, Double Choir, Organ and Orchestra*, ed. Denis Stevens (London: Novello, 1994)
T	Tenor

1

Introduction

With its mixture of the splendid and the intimate, the sensual and the sublime, the music of Monteverdi's *Vespro della Beata Vergine* (*Vespers of the Blessed Virgin*), often called the '1610 Vespers' for short, has gained widespread and enduring popularity. It was published, together with a Mass setting, in the *Missa ... ac Vespera ... cum nonnullis sacris concentibus* (*Mass and Vespers, with some Sacred Concertos*), which Monteverdi issued at Venice in 1610 (publication at Venice signifies not that it was a Venetian work, but that Venice was the main centre of music publishing in early seventeenth-century Italy). Like most late Renaissance publications of church music, this was a volume intended to serve a number of purposes. At one level, of course, it was a vanity publication, a portfolio of the composer's work gathered together for the world to admire, and the unprecedented way in which Monteverdi set out his Vespers music in the volume – as a set of music for Vespers of the Madonna interspersed with motets and the 'Sonata sopra Sancta Maria' – may have owed something to a wish to make the best possible show with a relatively small collection of settings.[1] At another level, however, it was intended as a resource book for choirmasters, who would have used as many or as few of the settings as they required or their singers could manage. With their needs in mind Monteverdi provided two paths for performance through the Vespers music: one requires a group of expert instrumentalists in addition to the vocal ensemble and organist; the other allows performance with organ alone. For this latter type of performance Monteverdi provided a second, six-part Magnificat in addition to the magnificent seven-part setting with instruments that is most often heard nowadays. As we shall see in Chapter 2, the 'sacred concertos' – the motets and the 'Sonata sopra Sancta Maria' – could have formed part of the celebration of Vespers in the seventeenth century, but equally they could have been omitted

1

altogether since none was integral to the official Vespers liturgy. And they could, if desired, have been used in other liturgical contexts or even as spiritual chamber music.

All this would have been well understood by musicians in the early seventeenth century, who would have accepted quite happily that the 1610 publication was a multi-purpose volume: there is not one possible '1610 Vespers' but several, and it is important to understand that to this extent Monteverdi's Vespers is not a work at all, but a group of works, not all of which were necessarily written at the same period. Most performances nowadays, however, even those that re-create the full liturgical context of a Vespers service, treat Monteverdi's 1610 Vespers at portfolio level and in their grandest dress, with a full complement of instruments: that is, they treat the collection as an artistic and liturgical unity.

Whether Monteverdi wrote his 1610 Vespers music simply for publication – an unlikely possibility, but one that cannot wholly be ruled out – or for performance in the north Italian city of Mantua, where he worked as choirmaster to Duke Vincenzo Gonzaga, he would not have envisaged the whole of it being performed in a concert version. Even though from 1609 the Gonzagas enjoyed concerts on Friday evenings in the Hall of Mirrors of the ducal palace, only a small proportion of the Vespers music – perhaps some of the smaller-scale motets – could possibly have featured in these. If the Vespers was ever heard as a complete unit during Monteverdi's lifetime it would have been in church, as an adornment of the Catholic liturgy. Monteverdi would have written his music with this in mind, and an appreciation of the 1610 Vespers in its liturgical context is essential to a full understanding of the 'work'. Equally, when analysing the musical settings of the psalms and Magnificat it is important to have some knowledge of the way in which psalms and canticles were customarily chanted in the Catholic Church since Monteverdi was set, or set himself, the challenging task of constructing a rich variety of settings based strictly on psalm tones, which are among the most limiting of plainsong formulae. Chapter 2, then, provides an introduction to the liturgy of Vespers and to plainsong psalmody, though this can be skipped on a first reading if it is found too technical.

The composition, publication and performance of the 1610 Vespers are surrounded by questions. Monteverdi was not employed at Mantua primarily as a church musician and the extent of his involvement in writing church music there is unknown. Why then, should he have produced such a magnificent volume of church music, and why in 1610? Was the music written over a period of time, or conceived for some grand Gonzaga celebration? Where was it first performed? Who were the musicians who sang and played it? Was it sung by a choir and soloists, or by an ensemble of solo singers? As we shall see, answers to these questions can be sought by decoding the information offered by the publication itself, by examining its production in the context of Monteverdi's career at Mantua and by interpreting the little documentation that survives. But it has to be admitted that most of the answers are, and are likely to remain, tentative.

It is exploration of these questions rather than analysis of the music itself that has occupied most writers on the 1610 Vespers. The only full-length study of Monteverdi's 1610 publication is Jeffrey Kurtzman's *Essays*, now out of print, though Kurtzman is about to publish a revised and extended version of his book, as well as a new edition of the Vespers. Analysis has tended to focus on formal aspects of Monteverdi's settings. This is understandable, since most of the ensemble pieces at least are based on verse-by-verse settings of psalm, hymn and canticle texts and some, like 'Dixit Dominus', are certainly based on abstract patternings. Nevertheless, Monteverdi did draw on his experience as a madrigalist in a number of the settings, finding musical metaphors for the imagery of the texts, sometimes on a small scale, sometimes taking a view of the text as a whole and once, in the case of 'Lætatus sum', providing a musical subtext (see below, Chapter 5, pp. 71–2).

The questions posed by Monteverdi's 1610 publication have exercised performers and historians for more than half a century, and some of the issues involved are still capable of provoking acrimonious debate. Answers to these questions, whether well founded or not, have influenced not only performances, but also editions of the music. This means that many editions of the Vespers, including some still available, do not represent Monteverdi's original print fully or reliably, but belong rather to the history of the reception and interpretation of the work and are discussed in Chapter 6.

A facsimile of the 1610 publication is available.[2] At the time of writing, however, only one generally available modern edition – by Jerome Roche[3] – can be recommended unequivocally as a study score. Roche's edition includes the full text of the Vespers, including the sacred concertos, both versions of the Magnificat and the organ score published in the *Bassus generalis* part-book. The text is presented in a clean and unfussy edition which preserves the visual aspect of Monteverdi's original notation while providing suggested solutions for the more difficult and controversial aspects of its interpretation.

There are other usable editions, though none in which it is quite as easy to follow all the material presented in this book. Clifford Bartlett has produced an excellent edition which has formed the basis of a number of recent performances.[4] Barring of duple-metre passages is by the semibreve rather than the breve which is the norm in the 1610 *Bassus generalis*; otherwise the visual aspect of the original notation is preserved. The edition lacks only the six-part setting of the Magnificat, which is, though, available on demand. And Denis Stevens's edition, first published in 1961, has recently been reissued to include the sacred concertos.[5] This edition has the advantage of being inexpensive, but it does not represent Monteverdi's text clearly. It was prepared for performance by choir and soloists and by players using modern instruments. Voice and instrumental names, note values and barring are altered and editorial tempi and dynamics added. The motet 'Nigra sum' is rescored from tenor solo to a dialogue for alto and tenor. Only the seven-part Magnificat is included. I have assumed that readers will have to hand one or other of these three editions. Unfortunately, however, the barring is different in each. In this book, bar numbers without a prefix refer primarily to the Roche edition; bar numbers in parenthesis and prefixed by Bt (Bartlett) or St (Stevens) refer to the other two editions where their barring differs.

Though Monteverdi's 1610 Vespers is a much loved 'work' it has also earned the more dubious distinction of provoking some of the most ill-tempered debate in the musicological literature. As Denis Arnold once amusingly put it:

> No doubt all professions have their hazards; and for the student of Monteverdi the principal one is surely that musicological Lorelei, the Vespers (of 1610, of course). To edit it is to receive the kiss of death as a

scholar. To perform it is to court disaster. To write about it is to alienate some of one's best friends. Even to avoid joining in the controversy is to find oneself accused of (i) cowardice, or (ii) snobbishness, or (iii) sitting on the fence, or (iv) all three.[6]

With this in mind, the present study is offered with some diffidence.

2

The 1610 settings and the liturgy of Vespers

Monteverdi's 1610 publication contains music for Mass and Vespers, the two services of the Roman Catholic liturgy that were most frequently supplied with elaborate musical settings in late sixteenth- and early seventeenth-century Italy. The Mass remains a central feature of the modern liturgy, though not in the form approved by the Council of Trent (the 'Tridentine' form) that Monteverdi would have known. The service of Vespers is, perhaps, less familiar, but some knowledge of its liturgy – that is, of the texts appointed by the Church to be said or sung at a Vespers service – is necessary not only for understanding why Monteverdi set the particular group of texts that he did, but also when evaluating various arguments about the contents of the 1610 print: arguments that have influenced both editions and performances of the music. And knowing how the psalms and Magnificat were customarily chanted in plainsong at Vespers is a valuable preliminary to analysing Monteverdi's settings, which make play with the ways in which his contemporaries would have expected to hear psalms sung in church. The first part of this chapter, then, provides a brief outline of Vespers, and Examples 1 and 2, below, can be used as a practical introduction to singing psalms in plainsong and *falsobordone* in conjunction with Appendix 2, which gives the texts and plainsongs of the psalms set by Monteverdi, using the same notational conventions. The appendix also begins the process of musical analysis by charting, verse by verse, the part(s) of Monteverdi's polyphonic settings in which the plainsongs appear.

Vespers: liturgy, plainsong, *falsobordone*

The evening service of Vespers was one of seven Offices (or Hours services) celebrated every day in Catholic religious communities during the Renaissance.[1] Like all the Offices its central feature was the singing of psalms – five in most cases – and at its culmination was the Magnificat – the canticle of the Blessed Virgin – during the singing of which the altar was ceremonially censed. The texts for all the Offices are found in a liturgical book called the Breviary, and texts and music in the Antiphoner and Psalter. The outline of Vespers, as celebrated on Sundays and feast days, when elaborate polyphonic settings would have been appropriate, is given in Table 2.1.

If Compline did not immediately follow Vespers, then the Marian antiphon appropriate to the season of the Church year – 'Alma redemptoris mater', 'Ave regina cœlorum', 'Regina cœli lætare' or 'Salve regina' – was sung with its associated devotions.[2]

Of the items in Table 2.1, only the texts of the first and last groups of versicles and responses, together with the Magnificat, remained constant for every celebration of Vespers. All the other texts varied according to the day of the Church calendar on which a specific Vespers service was celebrated. For feast days – such as days which commemorated events in the life of Christ, or the Blessed Virgin, or other saints – Vespers was celebrated twice, once on the evening preceding the feast (First Vespers) and once on the day itself (Second Vespers). Though the texts for First and Second Vespers of a given feast might be identical, generally their texts differed.

Some types of feast had texts in common. For example, at all Vespers of the Blessed Virgin the five psalms to be sung were those found in Monteverdi's 1610 publication – (A) 'Dixit Dominus' (Psalm 109; BCP 110),[3] (B) 'Laudate pueri' (112; BCP 113), (C) 'Lætatus sum' (121; BCP 122), (D) 'Nisi Dominus' (126; BCP 127) and (E) 'Lauda Ierusalem' (147; BCP 147, vv 12–20) – and the Office hymn was 'Ave maris stella'. The same five psalms were also appointed for Vespers on the feast days of other virgins and holy women, but the Office hymn differed according to the saint whose life was being celebrated. For Second Vespers of the feast days celebrating the apostles, on the other hand, the five psalms were (A) 'Dixit Dominus', (B) 'Laudate pueri', (C) 'Credidi', (D) 'In convertendo' and (E) 'Domine probasti me'.

As may be seen from the above, the psalms 'Dixit Dominus' and 'Laudate pueri' figure in Vespers for all these feasts. In fact, Vespers for all 'double' feasts (see below, p. 10) and Sundays of the year use a total of only fifteen different psalms,[4] a fact that allowed composers to

Table 2.1 The outline of Tridentine Vespers

Versicle [V]:	*Deus in adiutorium meum intende*
Response [R]:	*Domine ad adiuvandum me festina.*
Doxology:	*Gloria Patri, et Filio, et spiritui sancto.*
	Sicut erat in principio et nunc et sem-
	per, et in secula seculorum. Amen.
Alleluia:	*Alleluia.*

Antiphon (a)
Psalm (A)
Antiphon (a)

Antiphon (b)
Psalm (B)
Antiphon (b)

Antiphon (c)
Psalm (C)
Antiphon (c)

Antiphon (d)
Psalm (D)
Antiphon (d)

Antiphon (e)
Psalm (E)
Antiphon (e)

Chapter (short scriptural reading)

Hymn

Versicle and response

Antiphon (f)
Magnificat
Antiphon (f)

Collect (Prayer)

V: *Dominus vobiscum.*
R: *Et cum spiritu tuo.*
V: *Benedicamus Domino.*
R: *Deo gratias.*

produce publications of a reasonable size which could nevertheless claim to contain polyphonic settings for the whole year – publications like the *Sacra Omnium Solemnitatum Vespertina Psalmodia, cum Beatae Virginis Cantico* [i.e. the Magnificat], *6vv* (1593) and *Tutti li salmi che nelle solennità dell'anno al vespro si cantano, con duoi cantici della beata vergine* ... *8vv* (1601), of Giovanni Giacomo Gastoldi, who served as choirmaster of the ducal chapel of Santa Barbara, Mantua, during most of the years that Monteverdi was court choirmaster there.[5]

Monteverdi's 1610 collection would have had a more limited usefulness, though, as we have seen, its sequence of psalms was appropriate not only for feasts of the Blessed Virgin, but also for the feasts of other virgins and holy women; and individual items in the collection would have had a wider currency still: the opening 'Domine ad adiuvandum' and the Magnificat, for example, could have been used for Vespers on any major feast, providing, of course, that the choirmaster had at his disposal a group of singers capable of tackling elaborate polyphony.

The other variable elements of Vespers – the antiphons, the chapter, the versicle and response that precede the Magnificat, and the Collect – might also be common to more than one feast, but more important feast days were allocated texts specific (or 'Proper') to them alone; these are found in those sections of the Breviary and Antiphoner headed 'Temporale' (for Feasts of Our Lord) and 'Sanctorale' (Feasts of the Saints). By way of illustration, Appendix 1 shows a complete Second Vespers for the Feast of the Assumption of the Blessed Virgin, celebrated each year on 15 August.[6] The psalms and hymn are those common to feasts of the Blessed Virgin, while the antiphons (which on double feasts such as this were to be said or sung in full both before and after their respective psalms)[7] and other Proper elements relate more or less specifically to the concept of the Assumption – the Virgin's bodily ascent to Heaven. Some of the antiphons refer explicitly to this belief, but others express a more generalised devotion to the Virgin, like the antiphon to 'Lauda Ierusalem', which draws on the Song of Songs, the same biblical source from which the text of Monteverdi's 1610 motet 'Pulchra es' was taken. The antiphons thus form a specifically Christian frame for each of the Old Testament psalms.

In the Catholic liturgy, feast days are ranked according to their importance. The Tridentine breviary of 1568 established five classes of feast, with a further class – the 'Greater Double' – being added in 1602. These are, in descending order of importance:

Duplex i classis	Double of the first class
Duplex ii classis	Double of the second class
Duplex maius	Greater double
Duplex	Double
Semiduplex	Semi-double
Simplex	Simple[8]

In this ranking Vespers for the simplest feasts would have been sung to plainsong only, while the most important ones, which would have included the feast of the patron saint of a church, would have warranted the most elaborate music of which the church choir and instrumentalists were capable. When polyphonic settings of the liturgy were used at Vespers they functioned as substitutes for items that would otherwise have been sung in plainsong, though we should not assume that all the substitutable items in the service were actually performed in elaborate settings. So although Monteverdi provided a package of substitutes in his 1610 print he would not necessarily have expected to hear all performed in a single celebration of Vespers.

At sung Vespers, whether celebrated using plainsong alone, or a mixture of plainsong and polyphony, all the texts in Appendix 1 were set to music, producing a seamless sequence of music without verbal interruptions. The types of plainsong used for a celebration of Vespers for the Assumption of the Blessed Virgin are shown in the third column of the appendix, which also provides references to the locations of the plainsongs or plainsong formulae in a generally available source, the *Liber Usualis* (henceforth *LU*), a handy compendium produced at the beginning of the present century.[9]

In sources of plainsong melodies for Vespers, only the antiphons and hymn appear in a fully written-out form; the other texts were sung to formulae usually consisting of a reciting note, with inflections and cadences that parallel the punctuation of the text. Of these the simplest are the formulae for prayers and lessons. The formulae for chanting psalms and the Magnificat – the psalm tones – are rather more complex. One of them – Psalm Tone 8 – is given as Example 1(b), with three verses of the psalm 'Laudate pueri' underlaid, and the end of the

Ex. 1(a) antiphon

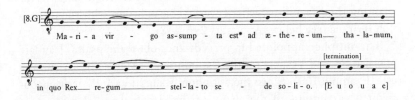

Ex. 1(b) psalm tone

doxology, the 'Gloria Patri ...', sung at the end of every psalm. Each verse is divided into two parts, marked by a cadence. The first part begins with an intonation (*intonatio*), the function of which is to lead smoothly from the final note of the preceding antiphon (shown as Example 1(a)) to the reciting note (the so-called 'tenor' of the mode; in this case C). The remaining syllables of the first half-verse are sung to the reciting note until the last accent is reached (shown in the example by the use of printed accents in the music, and underlining in the text), at which point the first cadence (the mediation or *mediatio*) begins. If the accent is followed by a single syllable, as in verse 2, then the final note of the cadence follows; if there are two or more syllables following the accent, as in verse 1, then the extra syllables are accommodated by the pitch shown as a void semibreve in the example.[10] Following the cadence, the singers observe a brief silence before beginning the second part of the verse, which starts directly on the reciting note and again moves to a cadence (*differentia* or *terminatio*) following the last accented syllable of the verse. In the case of this particular psalm tone there is also a melodic inflection for the two syllables that precede the accent. In showing where such inflections occur the convention is adopted here of printing such syllables in italics. Since the antiphon is not sung between the verses of the psalm, the second and subsequent verses begin directly on the reciting note, without the initial intonation. A different convention obtains for chanting the Magnificat, where every verse is begun with the intonation formula (see below, Appendix 2, p. 118).

The antiphon appointed to precede and follow the psalm 'Laudate pueri' at Second Vespers for the Assumption is 'Maria Virgo assumpta est' (Example 1(a)). Since the antiphon is sung to a fully written-out chant, the contours of the chant can be classified as belonging to a particular church mode, in this case Mode 8, with a final on G.[11] Since the mode of the antiphon is fixed, the appropriate psalm tone – Psalm Tone 8 – is chosen, to preserve modal unity (if the antiphon had been in Mode 6, then Psalm Tone 6 would have been used for the psalm text, and so on).

All Mode 8 antiphons end on G, so that only one intonation formula is needed to lead to the reciting note of Tone 8. However, when the psalm and doxology have been sung the antiphon has to be repeated and some means has to be found of providing a smooth transition from the end of the psalm tone to the beginning of the antiphon. In order to solve this problem, most psalm tones are provided with a variety of terminations, and the appropriate one chosen according to the note on which the antiphon begins. Psalm Tone 8, for example, is shown in *LU* (p. 117) with three possible terminations, two for use with antiphons beginning on G and one for use with antiphons beginning on C.

In *LU* the psalm tone and termination to be used with a particular antiphon are signalled twice: first, by a rubric at the beginning of the antiphon – in this case 8. G; and second, at the end of the antiphon, using a method found in earlier liturgical books, that is, by writing out the appropriate psalm-tone termination underlaid with the vowels of the last phrase of the doxology – 'e u o u a e' (= 'et in secula sEcU-lOrUm. AmEn' (see the end of Example 1(a) and the 'solution' at the end of Example 1(b)). In Appendix 1 the modes of the antiphons and psalm tones for the Assumption, together with the psalm-tone terminations, are shown in column 3, using the conventions of the *LU* rubrics.

A few further conventions need to be noted. The first is that the first part of each antiphon – up to the point marked by an asterisk in Example 1(a) – would have been sung over to one of the officiating clergy in order to establish the starting pitch; he would then have repeated the phrase and the choir would take over for the remainder of the antiphon. The first antiphon was begun by the duty priest, or the bishop (if present), and the subsequent ones by different clerics in an order laid down in the *Caeremoniale Episcoporum* (The Bishops' Ceremonial) of 1600. The first verse of each psalm would then have been started by one or more cantors and sung to the point shown by the asterisk in Example 1(b), the choir then taking over. And, in plainsong performances at least, the verses of the psalms would probably have been sung alternately by the two sides of the choir.[12]

The simplest form of polyphonic substitute for the plainsong psalm tones, and one that seems to have been widely used in late sixteenth-century Italy, was *falsobordone*, a chordal setting which, in its early stages at least, incorporated the psalm tone itself, usually in the uppermost voice or in the tenor. Such settings were particularly associated with the psalms for Sunday Vespers (Psalms 109–113) and, according to Murray Bradshaw, few settings survive for the Magnificat, perhaps because, since the Magnificat forms the climax of the service, a more elaborate treatment of its text was called for.[13] An example of a simple *falsobordone* for Psalm Tone 6 is shown in Example 2, drawn from a musical instruction book, Giovanni Battista Rossi's *Organo dei cantori* (*c.* 1585).[14] The text of the second verse of 'Dixit Dominus' has been underlaid in all four voices and the notation made to approximate to that used in Example 1. In this example the psalm tone is in the tenor voice. In performance, verses of the psalm set in *falsobordone* would probably have alternated with verses sung in plainsong, as shown in Example 2.

Bradshaw observed that there was a 'veritable explosion of publications' of *falsobordone* settings between 1580 and 1620. He attributed this not only to the increased use of part-music in churches with limited resources, but also to the fact that the simplicity of *falsobordone* reflected the view of the Council of Trent:

> Let all things be so restrained that ... everything, being produced clearly and perfectly, may peacefully reach the ears and hearts of the listeners ... the entire reason for singing [sacred texts] in musical strains ... is that the words might be comprehended by all and that the hearts of the listener might by joyful contemplation be seized with a desire of heavenly harmony and of blessed things.[15]

Ex. 2

He also noted a number of important changes in style and approach found in settings published from the 1570s onwards. These included extended cadence sections which involved extra notes being added to the psalm tone by the composer; the gradual abandonment of the psalm tone altogether; and an increase in the popularity of highly embellished *falsibordoni*, including pieces for accompanied solo voice.

Rome seems to have been the main centre of embellished *falsibordoni*, but some were also included in the *Cento concerti ecclesiastici* (1602) of Monteverdi's one-time Mantuan contemporary Lodovico Viadana.[16] Example 3 shows an elaborate *falsobordone* by Viadana for solo voice with continuo accompaniment, suitable for use with antiphons in Mode 6.[17] This example abandons the fixed reciting note of the psalm tone, but it retains the bipartite structure of the stricter type of *falsobordone* and a final cadence that leads smoothly to the repeated antiphon. It is this type of free *falsobordone* with extended cadences that Monteverdi employs, for example, in setting verses 2, 4, 6 and 8 of 'Dixit Dominus' (bars 12–24, 44–57, 75–83 and 104–13 respectively (Bt 23–45, 85–108, 144–59, 199–214)). But it is not only in this respect that Monteverdi's settings owe a debt to *falsobordone*: in their strict adherence to the psalm tones and the bipartite structure of the psalm verse, Monteverdi's 1610 psalm and Magnificat settings could all be said to be *falsibordoni* writ large.

Ex. 3

Problems posed by the 1610 Vespers

Falsobordone settings retained the flexibility of plainsong with respect to tonal agreement with the antiphon. Once a psalm tone with a single termination became embedded in a larger-scale polyphonic setting, however, this flexibility was lost, and in order to match polyphonic settings to the modes and terminations required by the antiphons for all the major feasts of the year, the late Renaissance choirmaster would, in theory at least, have needed access to an impossibly large library.

Some psalm collections were indeed organised to match the modes of the antiphons for particular feasts at a particular institution. Among the manuscripts of the ducal chapel of Santa Barbara at Mantua, for example, are several containing music by Gastoldi which are organised in this way, with the mode identified. One contains four-part psalm settings for Prime, Terce, Sext and None (but not Vespers) for the feast of St Barbara, the patron saint of the church; another contains Vespers psalms for a further ten groups of feasts.[18] However, when Gastoldi published psalms 'for all the solemn feasts of the year', he included only one setting of each psalm, just as Monteverdi did in publishing psalms for (all) Vespers of the Blessed Virgin. Collections of this kind, therefore, imply a break with the intimate relationship between the mode of the antiphon and the mode of the psalm setting. The individual items of Monteverdi's *Vespro della Beata Vergine* are shown in Table 2.2, together with the classification of the psalm tones and terminations that he uses, following the terminology of *LU*.

Table 2.2

Incipit	Vocal and instrumental forces (+ continuo)	Psalm tone and termination
Domine ad adiuvandum	6 voices + 6 instrumental lines	
Dixit Dominus	6 voices + 6 instruments	4E (4A in *LU*, which has the reciting note transposed from A to D.)
Nigra sum	1 voice	
Laudate pueri	8 voices	8G
Pulchra es	2 voices	
Lætatus sum	6 voices	2D
Duo Seraphim	3 voices	
Nisi Dominus	10 voices	6F
Audi cœlum	6 voices	
Lauda Ierusalem	7 voices	3a
Sonata sopra Sancta Maria	1 voice + 8 instruments	
Ave maris stella	7 voices + 5 instruments	
Magnificat	7 voices + 6 instruments	1D
Magnificat	6 voices	1D

No Marian Vespers liturgy has yet been discovered with antiphons that prescribe this sequence of tones and terminations for the psalms and Magnificat. This problem has provided one of the major bones of contention in discussions of the 1610 Vespers, and in this respect it is linked to a second problem, the question of what, if any, liturgical function is served by the motets and the 'Sonata sopra Sancta Maria' – the 'sacred concertos' as Monteverdi called them – which follow the psalm settings in the 1610 print.

One procedure, followed in Denis Stevens's editions of the Vespers, and (with the exception of the Magnificat antiphon) on the recordings by Jürgens (1966/67) and Bernius (1989), has been to choose antiphons with Marian associations that match the tones used in Monteverdi's psalm settings. This entails taking the antiphons out of their original liturgical contexts. In the case of Professor Stevens's editions they are drawn from Second Vespers of the Common of Feasts of the Blessed Virgin ('Dum esset rex', 'Læva ejus', 'Jam hiems transiit'), the Visitation ('Intravit Maria') and the Nativity of the Blessed Virgin ('Regali ex progenie', 'Gloriosæ Virginis'). Since this procedure does not respect liturgical propriety, however, it would not have found a place in the Church of Monteverdi and his contemporaries.

Another approach to the problem, foreshadowed by Leo Schrade and fully developed by Stephen Bonta,[19] proposed that the sacred concertos placed after the psalms in Monteverdi's print served as substitutes for the repeated antiphon, thus avoiding the problem of modal unity altogether. As Table 2.1 shows, however, the liturgy of Vespers does not call for the inclusion of motets or any other form of 'sacred concerto'. And the texts of Monteverdi's concertos do not correspond to those of the antiphons of any Marian feast in the Roman usage, despite occasional similarities. The sacred concertos are, then, non-liturgical, and a number of writers have taken the view that they did not warrant inclusion in a Vespers service.[20] And yet, by positioning each concerto after a psalm, a procedure which is not otherwise found in printed Vespers music before 1610, Monteverdi implied that they might serve at least a quasi-liturgical function, and that the collection as a whole was intended as a liturgical and artistic entity.

Bonta demonstrated that the Church sanctioned the use of organ music in place of the repeated antiphon, providing that its text was also recited clearly.[21] He referred to evidence of this practice provided in two seventeenth-century publications. In the 'Table drawn up for beginning organists of when and how long to play at Vespers with plainsong' in *L'organo suonarino*, a handbook for organists by the Bolognese organist and composer Adriano Banchieri, Banchieri stated that 'after the *sicut erat* [i.e. after the doxology] of each psalm has been finished [by the choir], one plays [for a] short or long [time] according to the occasion'. He also stated that 'After the Magnificat a *Franzesa Musicale* [a Capriccio] is played, or whatever else one wishes'; this practice is confirmed in Giovanni Battista Fasolo's *Annuale* (Venice, 1645), in which instrumental canzonas are provided to be played 'in place of the antiphon after the Magnificat'.[22] Bonta suggested that Monteverdi's motets and the 'Sonata sopra Sancta Maria', though texted, were intended to serve as antiphon-substitutes in a way analogous to instrumental or organ music. All are settings of texts appropriate to any Marian devotion, with the exception of 'Duo Seraphim', which has a Trinitarian text.[23] He also suggested that, since Monteverdi apparently provided no 'concerto' for use after the Magnificat, an instrumental piece should be played, as recommended by Banchieri and Fasolo. And finally, he suggested that, while the antiphon-substitute was sung or played the correct antiphon would have been said by one of the clergy in order to maintain the liturgical validity of the service.

And there the matter has rested for some twenty years, despite doubts expressed by James Armstrong, James H. Moore and Helmut Hucke.[24] There are two weaknesses, however, in Professor Bonta's argument. One is that while the idea of the concertos as antiphon-substitutes avoids the problem of modal unity between polyphonic psalm and repeated antiphon, it does not explain how modal unity was achieved between the first statement of the antiphon and the beginning of the psalm. In all probability the problem of modal unity was simply ignored and the antiphon sung to end on a pitch that would provide a reasonably smooth transition to the opening of the psalm.[25] But if this is true, then there is no reason why repeating the plainsong antiphon after the psalm should prove a much greater practical or theoretical problem. As Moore put it:

> While Banchieri, Fasolo and others give a prominent place to the discussion of mode in their manuals for organists, one must not forget that they are discussing services for plainchant choir and organ or, at their most elaborate, in *falsobordone* alternating with organ settings – all media for which the agreement of mode between psalms and antiphons would have posed no great problem. We really have no incontestable proof that such modal unity was necessary in services employing *canto figurato*, let alone those employing the more lavish forms of the *stile concertato*. This is not to say that psalms and antiphons would have been allowed to clash violently, but the agreement may have been a looser one than scholars have assumed.[26]

The other weakness in Professor Bonta's argument is that his evidence relates mainly to instrumental music and to music for the Mass. The idea of the concertos as antiphon-substitutes may seem a plausible one. But while organ music was officially permitted in place of the repeated antiphon, motets were not. The *Caeremoniale Episcoporum*, first promulgated by Pope Clement VIII on 14 July 1600, which had the effect of law within the Church, states quite clearly that at Vespers

> if it is wished, at the end of any psalm the antiphon may be repeated by the organ, but nevertheless the same antiphon must be repeated clearly by a Mansionarius or some other deputised person. And if there be anyone who wishes to sing with the organ, he shall sing nothing else but this same antiphon.[27]

This injunction is clear evidence of the importance of the antiphons in the liturgy of Vespers, where they provided a Christian context for the psalms. It could, of course, be argued that the injunction may have been breached, especially outside Rome. Monteverdi, however, prepared his 1610 publication with the intention of dedicating it to the pope and presenting it to him in person. His unprecedented placing of the sacred concertos after the psalm settings would surely have appeared very provocative to the Roman authorities if they had thought that he intended them as antiphon-substitutes in contravention of an injunction published only ten years earlier.

Closer examination of the wording of the injunctions contained in the *Caeremoniale Episcoporum* shows that while the ecclesiastical authorities were concerned that the repeated antiphon should not be omitted, whether said, sung in plainsong or sung to organ accompaniment, they did not explicitly forbid the use of extra-liturgical items between the end of one antiphon and the beginning of the next, so that one possible explanation for Monteverdi's apparent disregard of the Church's ban might be that he intended his sacred concertos to be sung in addition to the plainsong antiphons. Some, admittedly later, support for the idea that motets were used as additional, rather than substituted, embellishments of the Vespers liturgy comes from documents relating to Venetian practice. In 1639 the Venetian *Provveditori di Commun* decreed that in religious services celebrated in the *scuole* (the city's charitable confraternities) musical settings should not include

> transpositions in the order of words, or texts with made-up words which are not found in holy books, except that during the Offertory,

and the Elevation, and after the Agnus Dei [at Mass], and similarly between the psalms at Vespers ['alli Vespri, trà li Salmi'], one can sing motets on pious, devout texts which are taken from holy books.[28]

The practice of singing motets between psalms at Vespers was also observed on two occasions in Venetian churches by the young German composer Paul Hainlein, who visited the city in 1647. Of the first, he says:

between each psalm a sonata or a motet was performed ['Wirdt aber allezeit zwischen einen iedwetern psalm ein Sonata oder Motetten gemacht'], among them a Romanesca which a bass singer and his choir-boys sang with delightful style.[29]

On the second occasion he attended a Marian Vespers:

As regards music I heard some last Saturday in San Francesco [della Vigna] ... also on Sunday at Mass and then again at night, which began at 7 p.m. This was performed on the Feast of the Conception of Our Lady [8 December] when a platform was set up. The musicians on it consisted of 3 discant singers, 3 altos, 3 tenors and 3 basses in consort, also 4 violins, 2 *viole da brazzo*, 4 trombones, in ripieno 10 persons, 3 positives among which Signor Cavalli played.

The psalms were *Dixit Dominus*, *Laudate pueri*, *Lætatus sum*, *Nisi Dominus*, *Lauda Jerusalem*, also a hymn before the *Magnificat*, and after it *Alma redemptoris mater* [the seasonal Marian antiphon]. Between each psalm a motet or a sonata was given ['Aber zwischen jedweter psalm ein Motetten oder Sonata gemacht']. In one composition a bass and a treble singer from Rome sang a motet on the Virgin, with interpolated words from Psalm xlvi, about the destruction of the Turk's power, breaking his shield and bows, burning his warships and boats, and hurling his entire forces into the sea. There was also a monk who played solo violin, the like of which I have never heard before, unless it were one of the Emperor's violinists. The music was by Signor Rovetta.[30]

All three documents, then, seem to attest to a practice of singing motets or playing instrumental music *between* the psalms, rather than as antiphon-substitutes *after* each psalm. In this case, only four interpolated items would be needed between the five psalms. There is also some circumstantial evidence of this practice from an earlier Roman source. Felice Anerio's *Antiphonae, seu Sacrae Cantiones* of 1613 contains groups of pieces for various feasts, some of which are settings of antiphon texts, some of free motet texts. A group of four 'antiphons' is the norm for each feast, and in those cases in which genuine antiphon texts are set, they are the antiphons for the first four psalms, leaving the last presumably to be said or sung in plainsong.[31]

Monteverdi's 1610 print, of course, includes five concertos, of which the fifth is the 'Sonata sopra Sancta Maria', which is printed after the last psalm, 'Lauda Ierusalem'. Recently, however, David Blazey has argued very persuasively, and Andrew Parrott has supplied further evidence, that the text of the Sonata relates it to settings of the Magnificat antiphon 'Sancta Maria succurre miseris', which also uses a melodic phrase derived from the Litany of the Saints, so that, despite its (mis-)positioning in Monteverdi's print, it was in fact intended as an interpolated item after the Magnificat, where its rich instrumentation balances that of the seven-part Magnificat with instruments.[32] This makes for a very satisfactory musical, as well as liturgical, solution, since it places two of Monteverdi's most splendid settings at the climax of the Vespers service. Incidentally, these are also the two settings which have to be omitted if a performance of the Vespers is to be given without instruments other than the continuo. Monteverdi makes provision for this in his publication. The instrumental ritornelli in 'Dixit Dominus' are marked as optional, and those between the verses of 'Ave maris stella' can also be omitted; a second, six-part, setting of the Magnificat, with organ accompaniment, is provided at the end of the volume; and, perhaps surprisingly, the opening 'Domine ad adiuvandum' can also be performed without instruments: the single chord on which the choir chants for most of the movement is notated in all the part-books as though it were a *falsobordone* reciting note, the rests between phrases can easily be ignored, and only the 'Alleluia' is fully notated. The rhythm in which the response is to be chanted when instruments are used is shown only in the *Bassus generalis*, the part-book used by the director of the ensemble.

If Blazey is correct in suggesting that the Sonata should be performed after the Magnificat, then the position of the four remaining motets *between* the five psalms seems to relate the practice implied by Monteverdi's print to the practice implied by Anerio's *Antiphonae* and actual practice in Venice thirty years later. Perhaps, then, Monteverdi's *Vespro della Beata Vergine* is actually complete, and not lacking one antiphon-substitute. And perhaps the motets and Sonata are not antiphon-substitutes, but merely embellishments of the liturgy which are intended to be performed in addition to both statements of the antiphons. If the concertos are not antiphon-substitutes, but additional, extra-liturgical items, then it becomes easier to admit a Trinitarian text such as 'Duo Seraphim' within the context of a Marian Vespers.

We are left, however, with the question of why Monteverdi chose the particular psalm tones and terminations that he did. A significant clue to his choice of terminations can be found in the *Ragionamento di Musica*, a treatise published in 1587 by Pietro Pontio, a composer who worked at Parma, not far from Monteverdi's home city of Cremona. As a writer, Pontio concerned himself with practical matters, as well as theory, and his writings provide a number of insights into late Renaissance Italian modal usage in general, and Monteverdi's work in particular.[33] On pages 97–8 of the *Ragionamento* Pontio printed the eight psalm tones, showing each with one termination only (in *LU* terminology 1D, 2D, 3a, 4E, 5a, 6F, 7a, 8G): that is, with terminations corresponding to those used by Monteverdi (4E, 8G, 2D, 6F, 3a, 1D (see Table 2.2, above)). He then commented:

> It is true that these psalms have many and varied endings…but these, and likewise these openings and mediations now shown to you here, are those which composers are in the habit of using in their compositions, as you will be able to find, if you observe them.

Although Pontio's statement has yet to be tested, it does suggest that Monteverdi was simply following a common usage among composers of polyphonic psalm settings in choosing his psalm-tone terminations, rather than some unknown liturgical source. It may also be significant that he used only endings on the final of the mode or, in the case of Mode 3, on a note accepted as another principal cadential note.

Pontio's statement, then, provides further evidence of the decoupling of polyphonic psalm settings from the modes of plainsong antiphons in the late sixteenth century. And if the choice of psalm-tone termination had become a matter of compositional choice among composers, we might reasonably ask whether the same was true of the choice of mode. The idea that for each of his settings Monteverdi might have chosen the psalm tone for purely musical-compositional reasons is an intriguing one.

3

The 1610 print and Monteverdi's career

Monteverdi's *Vespro della Beata Vergine* was published while he was *maestro di cappella* at the Gonzaga court at Mantua in northern Italy. However, no performance of the Vespers, nor of any of its constituent parts, is known to have taken place at Mantua or, indeed, anywhere else during Monteverdi's lifetime; and there is little documentary evidence that relates directly to the composition and publication of the music. This is usual with respect to volumes of church music in the early seventeenth century, but it is often possible to relate such publications to the composer's career. At Mantua, however, Monteverdi was not, so far as we know, employed specifically as a church musician, and it is thus more difficult to account for his having produced a major collection of church music. The understandable frustration that this has caused for historians and performers alike has given rise to various hypotheses, some more solidly grounded than others, about why Monteverdi wrote and published this particular collection and why it takes the form that it does. Some of these can be evaluated fairly readily on the basis of documentary evidence, including the evidence of the publication itself, some require an understanding of the liturgical context, and others an understanding of circumstances in Monteverdi's career that might have prompted him to publish church music in 1610.

The 1610 publication

On 16 July 1610 Don Bassano Casola, Monteverdi's assistant as court choirmaster to Duke Vincenzo Gonzaga, wrote the following to Cardinal Ferdinando Gonzaga, the younger son of the duke, who was then resident in Rome:[1]

Monteverdi is having printed an *a cappella* Mass for six voices [the product] of great study and effort, he being obliged to handle continually, in every note through all the parts, building up more and more, the eight points of imitation [actually ten] which are in Gombert's motet 'In illo tempore'; and together with it he is also having printed some psalms of the Vespers of the Madonna with various and different manners of invention and harmony, and all on a *cantus firmus*, with the idea of coming to Rome this autumn to dedicate them to His Holiness.

The *Missa ... ac Vespera* was issued by the Venetian publisher Ricciardo Amadino probably in early September 1610 since Monteverdi dated his dedication from Venice on 1 September. Like most published polyphonic music of the period it was issued in part-books – in this case in seven books containing the parts for voices, string, wind and brass instruments, and an eighth book, called 'Bassus generalis' (General Bass) on its title-page and 'Partitura' (Score) in the printer's signatures.[2] This contains an almost entirely unfigured bass and, in the majority of cases, at least one further line drawn from the upper parts. These provide a guide for the organist and/or choirmaster and, since the more exposed vocal entries and virtuosic lines are usually reproduced, an opportunity to retrieve any false or missed entries.

The most unusual feature of the *Bassus generalis* is the printing out of all the 'fughe' – the points of imitation from Gombert's motet on which Monteverdi's Mass setting is based. These are of no practical use to the performer and must be there simply to draw attention to the compositional basis of the Mass, as though Monteverdi wished to underline its technical ingenuity. Similarly, the indication that the Vespers is 'composti sopra canti fermi' (composed on *cantus firmi*) is not strictly speaking necessary, but again draws attention to the technical basis of the settings. In other words, the *Bassus generalis* duplicates much of the information provided in Casola's letter. Moreover, though it was not unusual for early seventeenth-century volumes of church music to be brought out with full or short scores in addition to the continuo line,[3] the inclusion in the *Bassus generalis* of lines drawn from the upper parts makes it possible from that one book alone to grasp the essence of 'Domine ad adiuvandum', the psalms 'Laudate pueri' and 'Lætatus sum' and substantial sections of the Magnificat settings, and to read the entire scores of the motets 'Nigra sum', 'Pulchra es', 'Duo Seraphim', and the solo section of 'Audi cœlum', leaving no doubt that virtuoso singers and instrumentalists were required for a full performance of the Vespers music.

The seven vocal–instrumental part-books each measure about 22.5 x 17 cm and their title-pages are identical except for the different part-name – Cantus, Tenor, Altus, Bassus, Quintus, Sextus, Septimus – at the head of each page and the printer's signature (A, D, G, K, N, Q, T respectively)[4] following the date. The *Bassus generalis* was printed in a larger format, measuring about 34.5 x 24.5 cm. The title-pages of the vocal–instrumental parts read:

SANCTISSIMÆ
VIRGINI
MISSA SENIS VOCIBVS,
AC VESPERÆ PLVRIBVS
DECANTANDÆ,
CVM NONNVLLIS SACRIS CONCENTIBVS,
ad Sacella siue Principum Cubicula accommodata.

OPERA
A CLAVDIO MONTEVERDE
nuper effecta
AC BEATISS. PAVLO V. PONT. MAX. CONSECRATA.
[Coat of arms of Pope Paul V]
Venetijs, Apud Ricciardum Amadinum.
–––––––––
M D C X.

[To be sung to the most holy Virgin: a Mass for six voices and Vespers for more, with some sacred concertos – works suited to the chapels or chambers of princes, lately wrought by Claudio Monteverdi and dedicated to the most blessed Paul V, Pontifex Maximus.[5]]

On these title-pages, then, the layout and typography shows that the whole collection is in honour of the Virgin and suggests that the Mass is its most important item; the Vespers and sacred concertos[6] are grouped together through the use of small capitals. It also appears that the whole collection is intended for use in princely chapels or chambers (Monteverdi could equally well have been thinking of princes of the Church as of the secular prince by whom he was employed). A further phrase ('ad ecclesiarum choros'), clarifying the point that the Mass was also suitable for more general church use – that is, that it did not need the vocal and instrumental resources available to a prince –

was added to the title-page of the *Bassus generalis* – the book that an organist or choirmaster was likely to look at first, whether as performer or prospective customer – and the typography rearranged to distinguish between the newly added line, in small capitals, and the next two lines, which were elided and changed to upper- and lower-case letters:

SANCTISSIMÆ
VIRGINI
MISSA SENIS VOCIBVS,
AD ECCLESIARVM CHOROS
Ac Vespere pluribus decantandæ
CVM NONNVLLIS SACRIS CONCENTIBVS,
ad Sacella siue Principum Cubicula accommodata.

The remainder was left unchanged.

As Roger Bowers has pointed out, adding the new phrase makes the Latin more cumbersome (which argues in favour of its having been added as an afterthought); and it leaves a slight, and perhaps intentional, ambiguity over whether all the Vespers music was to be used in princely chapels or whether the concertos were simply spiritual chamber music.[7] Unfortunately, the new layout of the *Bassus generalis* title-page also has the effect of demoting the Vespers to a level of importance apparently much below that of either the Mass or the sacred concertos, an important point to note since it is this title-page alone that is usually discussed in studies of the Vespers, with misleading results. Denis Stevens, for example, used the differentiation in typography to reinforce his argument that the concertos were not part of the Vespers service.[8] Pierre Tagmann concluded, mistakenly, that

> the text of the *Vespro* is printed in the smallest possible type … in order to avoid offending the conservative Roman Curia; the crucial innovations were intended to a certain extent to be slipped in to the traditional framework through the back door, as it were.[9]

and Jeffrey Kurtzman that

> The appropriateness of the Mass and Vespers to Rome and Venice respectively may account for the much-noted difference in the size of the lettering of the two items on the title page.[10]

Monteverdi's dedicatory letter to Pope Paul V (Camillo Borghese) was printed in the vocal–instrumental part-books (but not in the *Bassus generalis*). It includes the customary extravagant compliments to the dedicatee and abasement on the part of the composer and need not be reproduced in full. One clause, however, is of interest. It reads

> and so that the mouths of Claudio's wicked detractors might be closed, I bring and offer at Your most holy feet these things of mine, such as they are, the fruits of my nocturnal labour.

The reference to 'wicked detractors' may be no more than the customary invocation of a patron's protection – Monteverdi had, indeed, printed a similar reference to 'malevolent tongues' in the dedication of his *Sacrae Cantiunculae* (Little Sacred Songs), published when he was only fifteen. On the other hand, by 1610 at least one of Monteverdi's detractors – Giovanni Maria Artusi – had been very voluble in print about his supposed shortcomings as a composer. If, on this occasion, Monteverdi meant his words to be taken literally, then they might provide part of the key to the whole enterprise.

By the beginning of October 1610 Monteverdi was in Rome with the intention of presenting the new volume to its dedicatee and of obtaining for his nine-year-old son Francesco a place at the Roman Seminary. His intention to visit Rome had been signalled officially as early as 4 September, when Prince Francesco Gonzaga wrote to his brother, Cardinal Ferdinando, recommending Monteverdi to his protection, saying (mistakenly) that he was coming to Rome to have some religious compositions published, and (correctly) that he wished to dedicate them to the pope; he asked Ferdinando to arrange a papal audience for Monteverdi.[11] On 7 October an official in Ferdinando Gonzaga's household wrote to Ferdinando to say that Monteverdi had already been in Rome for three days, staying at an inn without telling anyone of his arrival and that he had insisted that the composer move into Ferdinando's residence; Monteverdi was still in Rome on 30 October, when he was joined there by Bassano Casola. Evidently Duke Vincenzo Gonzaga had also written letters to Rome on his behalf, for two influential cardinals – Montalto and Borghese (the pope's nephew) – replied to the duke on 13 November and 4 December respectively, promising their support.[12] By 28 December at the latest Monteverdi was back in Mantua. His letter of that date to Ferdinando Gonzaga mentions that before leaving Rome he had heard Hippolita Marotta, one of Cardinal Montalto's singers, and that at Mantua he was compelled to assure another singer, Adriana Basile, 'how much the Most Illustrious Lords, cardinals Montalto and Borghese honoured and esteemed her'.[13] He had clearly, then, moved in the circles of both cardinals while at Rome.

No copy of the 1610 print survives in the Vatican Library, but a copy of the Altus part-book, bound in vellum and bearing the coat of arms of Pope Paul V, is located in the Archivio Doria Pamphili in Rome, and probably belonged to a set presented to the pope by Monteverdi. A manuscript copy of the Mass is located in the Vatican (Biblioteca Apostolica Vaticana, Cappella Sistina MS 107). According to Jeffrey Kurtzman this is the work of a copyist and contains the same dedication as the 1610 print as well as the ten 'fughe'.[14]

In his 1610 publication, then, Monteverdi seems to have been concerned to project an image of himself as an expert composer capable of working with the traditional materials of Catholic Church music in the spirit of the Counter-Reformation. His Mass setting which, as we know from Casola's letter, was the product of 'great study and effort', is an essay in the respected 'prima prattica' style of Roman church music and, moreover, one intended to demonstrate his expertise through the use of a difficult form of parody technique. The Vespers, 'composed on *cantus firmi*', reinforces this image, though it also shows how traditional plainsongs could be combined with the most up-to-date styles of virtuoso court music. Moreover, the consistent use of *cantus firmi* gives the impression that the Vespers had been planned as a unit, illustrating the variety of invention possible within an apparently limited framework. Monteverdi's decision to dedicate the volume to the pope was taken, perhaps, in the hope of obtaining a place for his son at the Roman Seminary. However, as we have seen, his journey to Rome to present the volume also allowed him to make himself known in influential Roman circles.

There are several questions on which the direct documentary evidence is silent. It does not tell us, for example, whether any of the music was performed before publication; nor does it tell us unequivocally whether it was composed shortly before publication, nor whether it was composed as a unit or as a series of individual pieces written over a period of several years. There is nothing to tell us why Monteverdi composed the music, only a few hints as to why he published it, and no evidence of any performance following publication. It is possible to explore most of these questions using indirect evidence of various kinds, and the remainder of this chapter will be concerned with explorations of this kind. But we have to recognise that, enjoyable though they may be, the hypotheses to which these explorations give rise remain hypotheses and not established facts.

Monteverdi and church music at Mantua

First, what evidence is there that Monteverdi was involved in performing or composing church music at Mantua? As far as composition is concerned, the only concrete evidence is the 1610 publication itself, and Monteverdi's letter of 26 March 1611 to Prince Francesco Gonzaga, with which he enclosed a 'Dixit Dominus' for eight voices, a motet for two voices to be sung at the Elevation (i.e. during Mass), and a Marian motet for five voices.[15] Documents suggesting that he might have been engaged with church music at an earlier date are few and far between.

Monteverdi had come to Mantua probably between 1590 and 1591 as part of a more general expansion of the court's musical staff (its 'cappella') begun by Vincenzo Gonzaga soon after he succeeded to the duchy in August 1587.[16] He was clearly viewed by Vincenzo Gonzaga as a useful and versatile musician, and when the duke journeyed to Hungary between June and November 1595 on a military expedition against the Turks he took Monteverdi with him as *maestro di cappella* in charge of a group of singers. At the Imperial camp this group was responsible for performing both sacred and secular music, promoting the image of Vincenzo Gonzaga as a liberal Catholic prince. As Fortunato Cardi, chronicler of the expedition, wrote:

> His Highness often sumptuously banqueted many lords and barons of the army, who for the better part of the day would come to pass the time in a friendly manner with His Highness, on whose order not just on feast days but every day four or five Masses were said in his quarters, and he lived in a Catholic manner, but on the solemn [days] Vespers was sung with music by singers and an organ which he had brought with him, to the infinite pleasure not, I say, of those who were serving His Highness, but of other Catholics in the army, who gathered there.[17]

The repertory of Vespers music that the group performed is uncertain, though it may have consisted of little more than plainsong and *falsobordone* psalm settings and motets for a few voices with organ. It is likely that Monteverdi sang with the group, as well as acting as its *maestro*, and possibly its organist.[18] Whether any of the 1610 settings date from these years is a moot point.

This is the first and the only secure information that we have of Monteverdi's performing church music for Vincenzo Gonzaga. When he applied to be promoted, however, in a letter of 28 November 1601, he couched his application in terms which embraced sacred as well as secular music.[19] His letter suggests, for one thing, that he had applied for the post of organist of the ducal chapel of Santa Barbara on the death of Francesco Rovigo in 1597. He now asked for the appointment formerly held by Giaches de Wert, and to be *maestro* 'both of the chamber and of the church'. This may mean that he was asking to be given control both of the court *cappella* and that of Santa Barbara, despite the fact that in 1601 Giovanni Giacomo Gastoldi still held the title of *maestro* of Santa Barbara. Though Monteverdi was made court choirmaster, which may have involved directing and composing some church music, his apparent request to be put in charge of Santa Barbara was not granted. (A later request to be employed only as a church musician at Mantua, made in 1608, was likewise rejected (see below, p. 37)). Lastly, he expressed a wish to have greater opportunity for composing motets and Masses for the duke. This suggests that he had written little or no sacred music during his first decade at Mantua. Admittedly, little is known about this period of his work, and only nine of his letters survive from the period before 1610. Such evidence as there is, however, suggests that Monteverdi was mainly involved in secular music both before and after his appointment as *maestro di cappella*.

Three theories

Since it cannot be shown that Monteverdi was regularly active as a church musician at Mantua, theories on the genesis and first performance of the 1610 Vespers music have generally concentrated on suggesting particular occasions for which he might have written the Vespers. One possibility, first suggested by Pierre Tagmann, is that the Vespers might have been written to celebrate the birth of Francesco Gonzaga's daughter Maria (29 July 1609) and performed on an appropriate Marian feast following this date – perhaps on 25 March 1610, the Feast of the Annunciation and Maria Gonzaga's name day.[20]

Two other theories require some knowledge of the Mantuan context. The duchy that Vincenzo Gonzaga inherited was one of the most richly endowed in northern Italy, and the ducal palace one of the largest in Europe; within it there were some five family chapels.[21] In 1561 Duke Vincenzo's father, Guglielmo Gonzaga, had begun building the basilica of Santa Barbara, a palace chapel on a grand scale dedicated to the patron saint of the Gonzaga family.[22] The basilica was completed in 1564, but remodelled and enlarged between 1569 and 1572. Its design is interesting. The high altar was placed at the centre of an apse at the East end and, unusually, the celebrant at Mass faced the congregation while the remaining clergy, including those responsible for singing plainsong, sat behind the altar. When polyphony was performed, however, the musicians were situated in a gallery at the West end of the church.

Guglielmo Gonzaga's plans for Santa Barbara were not limited to its architecture and clerical establishment. By dint of considerable persistence he also managed to establish for it a liturgy distinct from that of Rome, together with a body of reformed plainsong, both of which were developed under his personal supervision. The Santa Barbara breviary and missal were finally published with papal approval in 1583, with the injunction that they were to be used only within Santa Barbara itself.

Santa Barbara was a collegiate church directly under the authority of Rome. In the late sixteenth and early seventeenth centuries its establishment consisted of about sixty people including an organist and between six and eight professional singers.[23] From 1564 to 1596 overall control of its music was vested in Giaches de Wert, who also acted as court choirmaster. From 1592, however, Giovanni Giacomo Gastoldi acted as *maestro di cappella* of Santa Barbara, though he was apparently still overseen by Wert. After Wert's death the two posts seem to have been definitively separated. Gastoldi continued as *maestro* at Santa Barbara until his death in January 1609, when he was succeeded by Antonio Taroni (1609) and Stefano Nascimbeni (1609–12), while the position of court choirmaster went successively to Benedetto Pallavicino (1596–1601) and Monteverdi (1601–12).

After Santa Barbara was built the cathedral of San Pietro, at which court musicians had also served, became effectively separated from the court musical establishment. Two other Mantuan churches, however – Sant'Andrea and the Jesuit church Santissima Trinità – continued to be used by the Gonzagas for ceremonial purposes. It was at Sant' Andrea on Sunday 25 May 1608 that Vincenzo Gonzaga inaugurated the wedding celebrations for his son Francesco and Margherita of Savoy by instituting a new order of chivalry in honour of Christ the Redeemer and installed Francesco as its first member. Following this ceremony solemn Vespers was sung, presided over by the Bishop of Mantua. Iain Fenlon has suggested that the 1610 Vespers may have been written for, and performed at this occasion.[24] It is true, as critics of Fenlon's theory have pointed out, that a Vespers of the Blessed Virgin would have been liturgically inappropriate to a ceremony celebrating Christ the Redeemer. Nevertheless, since certain elements are common to all celebrations of Vespers (see above, pp. 7ff.), it is possible that individual movements might have been used: the re-sounding 'Domine ad adiuvandum', for example, or the seven-part Magnificat, both of which include music derived from Monteverdi's opera *Orfeo*, which had been commissioned by Prince Francesco in 1607.

If we assume that the Vespers was performed, in whole or in part, at Mantua, then Santa Barbara seems an obvious location for such a performance. Objections have been raised to this idea. As we have seen, Monteverdi was never in charge of music at Santa Barbara, and none of his church music survives in its library; indeed, the normal repertory of the basilica seems to have been rather conservative in style.[25] Objections have been raised on other grounds, too. In an influential article, Knud Jeppesen claimed that the sequence of psalms set by Monteverdi could not have been used for Vespers at Santa Barbara.[26] He supported his argument by showing that Monteverdi's psalms did not match those appointed for First Vespers of the Visitation of the Blessed Virgin in the Santa Barbara breviary,[27] though they did correspond to those set for the same service in the Roman *Antiphonale* published in 1912. He also stated that the 'Ave maris stella' melody used by Monteverdi in 1610 corresponded more closely to the plainsong published in the Roman *Antiphonale* than to examples of the melody that he had found in Manuscripts 8, 9 and 11 of the Santa Barbara Library.

In fact, Jeppesen's article is very misleading. He was correct in stating that in the Mantuan rite, unlike the Roman, the psalms for First Vespers of the Visitation do not correspond to the female *cursus* set by Monteverdi. He was wrong, however, to generalise from this particular case. For Second Vespers of the same feast in the Santa Barbara breviary the female *cursus* is quite explicitly prescribed, as it is also for Second Vespers of the Feast of the Conception of the Blessed Virgin (8 December), the other Marian double feast in the Santa Barbara calendar.[28] Three more Marian feasts are classified as Major Doubles: the Purification (2 February), Annunciation (25 March) and Assumption (15 August). In the Mantuan breviary the rubrics for these feasts are not easy to follow, but use of the female *cursus* seems to be confirmed by a group of four-part psalm settings for Second Vespers of the Purification by Giovanni Giacomo Gastoldi which survives in manuscript in the Santa Barbara collection and includes settings of 'Nisi Dominus' and 'Lauda Ierusalem', and a similar group of settings exists for Vespers of the Assumption and Second Vespers of the Annunciation which includes 'Laudate pueri', 'Lætatus sum', 'Nisi dominus' and 'Lauda Ierusalem'.[29] Monteverdi's settings, then, could also have been used at Santa Barbara for Second Vespers on any of these major feasts.

Jeppesen's observation on the 'Ave maris stella' melody again generalises too readily from limited evidence. The melody of 'Ave maris stella' exists in a number of variants; and the Roman *Antiphonale* of 1912 is not a reliable guide to late sixteenth- or early seventeenth-century sources. Three versions of the hymn melody are given in Appendix 2 (pp. 116–17), for comparison with the version set by Monteverdi. Melody (b) shows versions found in two Santa Barbara manuscripts – MSS 9 (f. 48^V) and 11 (ff. 21^V and 48^V), the *Proprium Sanctorum* for the periods December–June and June–August respectively. Even here there is a variant – the added C in the second phrase found in MS 11, f. 48^V. Melody (c) is a version found in a late sixteenth-century Roman psalter-hymnal; melody (d) is from the *Antiphonale* of 1912. Despite Jeppesen's assertion, it is the Santa Barbara versions of the plainsong that bear the closest resemblance to Monteverdi's melody.[30] To draw any firm conclusions from this limited evidence alone, however, would be to fall into the same trap that befell Jeppesen. Moreover, as is shown in the introduction to Appendix 2, most of the variants in the texts set by Monteverdi are found in both Roman and Santa Barbara sources, suggesting that they would have been acceptable in either context, while the evidence of ligature variants in the psalm tones is inconclusive.

The lack of copies of Monteverdi's music in the Santa Barbara library seems puzzling at first, but may well indicate that the library includes only music used in the basilica's regular round of services. Since Monteverdi was not employed at the basilica his music, if used at all, would probably have been employed only on special occasions when the musicians of Santa Barbara were joined by the instrumentalists and singers (not least the virtuoso castrato sopranos) of the court *cappella*. These occasions might have included feasts of the Virgin but, as Graham Dixon has pointed out, they would certainly have included the grandest celebration of the year, for the feast of St Barbara, the basilica's patron saint.[31] The feast of St Barbara is ranked as a Greater Double in the Santa Barbara calendar and stands at the head of the *Proprium Sanctorum* in the Santa Barbara breviary; and the psalms specified for Second Vespers of the feast are those of the female *cursus*, as set by Monteverdi.[32] Moreover, the fact that Gastoldi omitted the psalms for Second Vespers from his manuscript collection of four-part psalms for the Offices of St Barbara's day suggests that this service was provided with special music.[33] All the settings of Monteverdi's 1610 Vespers, with the exception of 'Audi cœlum' and 'Ave maris stella', and the possible exception of the 'Sonata sopra Sancta Maria' (which would become the 'Sonata sopra Sancta Barbara'), are as appropriate for the feast of St Barbara as for feasts of the Virgin; indeed, the Trinitarian text of 'Duo Seraphim' is more appropriate for St Barbara, who was martyred for her belief in the Trinity.

If we assume that Monteverdi did not write the music of the 1610 Vespers simply for publication, then Dixon's idea that its music may have been written for celebrations of St Barbara's day at Mantua is a very plausible and attractive one, and it allows for the music to have been written over a number of years, rather than for a single occasion. Moreover, in their rigorous adhesion to the psalm tones, Monteverdi's settings are similar to the church music of Gastoldi, choirmaster of Santa Barbara, whose published psalm settings make extensive use of *falsobordone*; they may, thus, owe something in this respect to a Santa Barbara tradition.

If some, or all, the settings of Monteverdi's 1610 Vespers did, indeed, originate from celebrations of the feast of St Barbara at Mantua, it is not difficult to account for his having marketed them as Vespers of the Blessed Virgin. The feast of St Barbara was important only in those churches of which she was patron saint: in the Roman calendar it was not even ranked as a double feast; the Blessed Virgin, on the other hand, was universally venerated, and several of her feasts were ranked at a level which warranted elaborate polyphony. A set of Vespers psalms for feasts of the Virgin would, therefore, have enjoyed a greater chance of selling.

It has sometimes been argued that the conservative style of the 1610 Mass represents Monteverdi looking to Rome, while the more 'advanced' style of the Vespers represents his looking to Venice.[34] However, the Vespers settings are not specifically Venetian in style. Their conception as large-scale *falsibordoni* is both Mantuan and Counter-Reformation in spirit, and there is no reason to suppose that they would have been unwelcome in the major churches of Rome, which was a centre of virtuoso singing, or, indeed, for the pope's 'secret' (i.e. personal) Vespers.[35]

Motives for publication

Although Monteverdi was never appointed choirmaster of Santa Barbara, he did make two requests to be appointed to the post, the second in an apparently desperate attempt to free himself from what he had come to see as the tyranny of the demands made upon him by the Gonzagas for entertainment music. It is in the circumstances surrounding this second bid for the appointment in 1608 that we can glimpse a possible reason for his decision to publish the 1610 volume, though in order to understand the context fully we must look further back in his career.

While we know little about Monteverdi's activity as a composer of church music at Mantua, it is clear that he was active as a composer of secular music even during the 1590s. His third book of madrigals was published in 1592, and 'Ah, dolente partita' was printed in Germany in 1597. Other madrigals were circulating in manuscript by the last years of the century. Some of them were heard in Ferrara in 1598 by Giovanni Maria Artusi, a canon regular of SS. Salvatore, Bologna. In his *L'Artusi, overo Delle imperfettioni della moderna musica* (The Artusi, or Of the Imperfections of Modern Music) (Venice, 1600) Artusi criticised nine examples from three madrigals by Monteverdi which were published only later, in the fourth and fifth books of madrigals (1603 and 1605 respectively). He was most censorious about what he saw as Monteverdi's breaking of established rules by using exposed and unprepared dissonances, a practice which he contrasted with that of composers like Lassus and Palestrina.[36]

A second volume also containing criticism of Monteverdi's music appeared from Artusi's pen in 1603.[37] Monteverdi replied in a preface to his fifth book of madrigals (1605), robustly defending his compositional methods and saying that the techniques to which Artusi objected represented a Second Practice (*seconda pratica*) quite different from the *prima pratica* of Lassus and Palestrina. This preface was reprinted in his *Scherzi musicali* of 1607 with glosses by his brother, Giulio Cesare Monteverdi, which made clear that Monteverdi's 'irregular' dissonance usage was inspired by the meaning and emotions of the texts that he set. In responding to Artusi, then, Monteverdi declared himself an unashamed modernist.

Giulio Cesare's glosses in the preface to the *Scherzi musicali* were prompted by a further pamphlet attacking Monteverdi that had appeared from an author writing under the pseudonym Antonio Braccino da Todi. No copy of this pamphlet survives, but a second, from the same author and attacking Monteverdi yet again, appeared in 1608, under the title *Discorso secondo musicale* (Venice, 1608). From this it is apparent that Antonio Braccino knew Artusi if, indeed, he was not Artusi himself. This time, however, Monteverdi made no direct response and his silence may have been prompted by a change in his own circumstances. On 10 September 1607 his wife Claudia had died, leaving Monteverdi with two young children to care for under chronically straitened financial circumstances. Only a fortnight later, however, he was recalled to court to begin work on music for the celebrations to follow the marriage of Francesco Gonzaga to Margherita of Savoy in 1608. For these Monteverdi wrote the opera *Arianna*, under great pressure, probably within the space of two or three months, plus the *Ballo delle Ingrate* and a prologue for Guarini's play *Idropica*, setting, by his own reckoning, some 1500 lines of poetry. He had also to rehearse and direct the music for the festivities.

The experience took a severe toll of his health and morale. He left Mantua for his father's house in Cremona, from where his father, acting as his mouthpiece, wrote to Vincenzo Gonzaga on 9 November 1608, saying that Monteverdi had arrived in Cremona seriously ill, burdened with debts, and asking that he might be discharged from the duke's service 'so that he can find other air for his health and less trouble, and another fortune for the well-being of his poor sons'. He continued:

> Whenceforth I turn yet again to beseech you that by Christ's heart you permit him the requested discharge, assuring Your Most Serene Highness that all his well-being he will always recognise as coming from your generosity, for if from the favour of your generous dismissal it happens that he serves a prince, I know that in this respect he will be viewed favourably. If Your Most Serene Highness commands only that he serves in the church, that he will do, for even from this source he will draw 400 *scudi* as a fixed income and 150 as extras, from which he will be able to advance something for his sons, availing himself also of me if the need arises.[38]

Having received no reply, Baldassare Monteverdi wrote again on 26 November, this time to the duchess, but to no avail. On 30 November Monteverdi received a letter from a court official, Annibale Chieppio, ordering him back to Mantua to begin work on new theatrical music. He responded in a controlled but deeply bitter letter in which he complained of the treatment that he had received during the 1608 wedding festivities, comparing his poor financial reward with those of other musicians of similar status, and finally asking again to be discharged from his duties at Mantua.[39] This was not granted.

Baldassare Monteverdi's letter of 9 November 1608 illustrates the quandary in which Monteverdi found himself. Soured by the experience of the preceding year, he wished to leave Vincenzo Gonzaga's service. However, he knew that unless the duke released him he would be unable to find a post as court choirmaster to another nobleman. As an alternative he requested to be allowed to serve only as a church musician, which he saw as representing a lighter burden of work for which he would be generously and regularly paid. In this respect he may again have had in mind being appointed choirmaster of Santa Barbara, for Gastoldi was by now seriously ill (he died in January 1609). As in 1601, though, his request was unsuccessful.

In reflecting upon his position Monteverdi must have realised that his best hope for a secure future outside Mantua was as a church musician. In this respect, however, he was not well placed to find a post of any importance. His growing reputation as a composer had been forged in the field of the madrigal and theatre music: he had no substantial publication of church music to his credit. Moreover, he had been accused of being a composer whose style undermined the foundations of acceptable musical technique. His public confrontation with Artusi and Braccino, while of no consequence to his work as a court composer, might well have raised doubts in the minds of ecclesiastical authorities, particularly in Rome, which was, after all, where most major church posts were to be found. Considerations such as these might well have prompted Monteverdi to make no verbal reply to Braccino's *Discorso secondo* of 1608, but instead to issue a collection of church music that would demonstrate not only his considerable musical gifts, but also that he was capable of writing a Mass in *prima pratica* style – and a particularly learned example at that – and Vespers music based on the authority of plainsong.

Several other aspects of the 1610 print make sense in this light. The idea of presenting the Vespers psalms and sacred concertos as a 'Vespers of the Blessed Virgin', though not unique, had the advantage of making maximum impact with a relatively limited quantity of music, and the design of this part of the collection, beginning and ending with large-scale pieces scored for voices and instruments,[40] and with the sacred concertos interleaved between the psalms, and arranged in ascending order of the number of the forces required, reinforces the sense of a grandiose conception presented for the contemplation and admiration of the beholder. It is precisely this aspect of the 1610 Vespers – as a well-organised portfolio designed to demonstrate Monteverdi's invention and craftsmanship – that justifies performing them nowadays as though they were a concert work rather than a collection of individual pieces which can be lifted out of context for use in the liturgy.

Monteverdi's decision to dedicate the volume to the pope might also be seen as part of his plan, since the dedication, once accepted, implied papal acceptance of the music within the volume – a powerful antidote to the criticisms of Bolognese canons! It also gave Monteverdi an excuse to journey to Rome in order to present the volume personally; and though we need not assume that he actively searched for a post at Rome between October and December 1610 he may have hoped that his visit there, which allowed him to move in the circles of influential cardinals, perhaps performing his own music, would ensure that his name was remembered should a post become vacant. Any suspicions that the Gonzagas might have entertained were answered by Monteverdi's using the visit to attempt to place his son in the Roman Seminary.

When were the Mass and Vespers written? Bassano Casola's reference to the 'great study and effort' that the Mass had cost Monteverdi suggests that it, at least, had been written recently. The sacred concertos, with the possible exception of the 'Sonata sopra Sancta Maria', might have been written over a number of years as part of Monteverdi's palace duties: they could, after all, have been written for use in the small palace chapels, as motets in the celebration of Mass as well as Vespers, or they might have been written for extra-liturgical performance – for Vincenzo Gonzaga's spiritual refreshment. As far as the other Vespers settings are concerned there are several possibilities: (1) that Monteverdi had a substantial stock of settings written over a period of up to twenty years, from which he chose the finest of his work; (2) that he wrote all, or most of the settings for a specific occasion; (3) that he wrote all, or most of the settings specifically for publication, probably after 1608. (The opening response and the seven-part Magnificat were almost certainly written after 1607 since they incorporate music from Monteverdi's opera *Orfeo* of that year.) The *cantus firmus* technique that Monteverdi employs so consistently for the psalms and Magnificat settings argues a unified conception. On the other hand, since there seems to have been a tradition of *cantus firmus* psalm settings written for Santa Barbara, Monteverdi's psalms might have been written at various times and their appearance of unity may be misleading. At present the question cannot be resolved satisfactorily, though it has to be said that we have no evidence that Monteverdi was involved in writing large-scale church music during the earlier part of his career at Mantua.

Whatever may have motivated Monteverdi to publish the 1610 book, its value was to be proved within a very few years. On 18 February 1612 Duke Vincenzo Gonzaga died. His successor, Duke Francesco, inherited a court whose finances had been severely undermined by his father's prodigality. Among the many servants that he dismissed were Monteverdi and his brother Giulio Cesare, who had unwisely chosen to hint that they could obtain better employment elsewhere.[41] Following his dismissal from Mantua Monteverdi languished for more than a year without regular employment and he was extremely fortunate that in 1613 Giulio Cesare Martinengo, *maestro* of St Mark's, Venice, died, leaving an important church post vacant. He was auditioned for the post on 1 August 1613. His audition consisted of directing a Mass with instrumental accompaniment at St Mark's which he had previously rehearsed at the church of San Giorgio Maggiore.[42] The 1610 Vespers did not play a direct part in his audition.[43] In their report signalling Monteverdi's appointment as *maestro di cappella* at St Mark's, however, the procurators made clear that they had taken into account not only Monteverdi's performance but also his published works:

> Claudio Monteverde, formerly *maestro di cappella* of the Lord Duke Vincenzo and Duke Francesco of Mantua, is commended as a most outstanding individual. Their Most Illustrious Lordships are further confirmed in this opinion of his quality and virtue both by his works which are found in print and by those which today Their Most Illustrious Lordships have sought to hear to their complete satisfaction in the Church of St Mark with its musicians. Therefore they have balloted and voted in unanimous agreement that the aforesaid Claudio Monteverde should be appointed *maestro di cappella* of the Church of St. Mark.[44]

Whether by accident or design, then, the 1610 publication played a part in securing Monteverdi's future in an important post and one that seems to have brought him enduring satisfaction.

4

'*Suited to the chapels or chambers of princes*'

Monteverdi's comment that the Vespers settings and sacred concertos were 'suited to the chapels or chambers of princes' indicates that he expected his music to be performed by the expert singers and instrumentalists employed at a court like Mantua or at major churches like St Peter's, Rome, or St Mark's, Venice, or perhaps in one of the musical establishments presided over by a cardinal. And since court and Church were the major employers of professional musicians in the late Renaissance, such establishments would have included the finest performers of the day. The sacred concertos of the 1610 print were certainly designed to show off the accomplishments of such performers, and the styles and techniques that they exemplify range from well-established traditions of vocal and instrumental virtuosity to the most up-to-date rhetorical styles of Florentine continuo song and opera.

Virtuoso singers were highly prized in court circles, the best of them receiving much higher payment than the composers who supplied them with music. Unlike the star singers of today, however, whose voices are trained to produce a rich, dark, powerful tone that can be projected over a large orchestra, virtuosos of Monteverdi's day cultivated lighter and more flexible voices with the ability to articulate notes very rapidly in the throat.[1] This last ability was particularly important since they were expected, especially when singing solo, to grace the lines that they sang with ornate and technically difficult improvised ornamentation; and their ability to do this was one of the most admired aspects of their art.[2] The most agile singers of this period were apparently able to articulate clearly, and without any slackening of the basic tempo,[3] semiquaver and even demisemiquaver ornamentation of the kind written out, for example, in bars 8–18 (Bt & St 15–28) of Monteverdi's 'Duo Seraphim'.[4]

The best-known account of virtuoso singing in the late Renaissance is Vincenzo Giustiniani's vivid description of the professional women singers employed at the courts of Ferrara and Mantua. His account makes clear not only that the ladies cultivated an expressive, rhetorical manner of singing using rubato and dynamic contrast, but also that unlike earlier virtuosi they used ornamentation judiciously so that it did not obscure the text:

> The ladies of Ferrara and Mantua were highly competent, and vied with each other not only in regard to the timbre and disposition of their voices but also in the design of exquisite passages [*passaggi*] delivered at opportune points, but not in excess (the falsetto Giovanni Luca [Conforto] of Rome, who served also in Ferrara, usually erred in this respect). Furthermore, they moderated or increased their voices, loud or soft, heavy or light, according to the demands of the piece they were singing; now slow, breaking off sometimes with a gentle sigh, now singing long passages legato or detached, now *gruppi*, now leaps, now with long trills, now with short, or again with sweet running passages sung softly, to which one sometimes heard an echo answer unexpectedly. They accompanied the music and the sentiment with appropriate facial expressions, glances and gestures, with no awkward movements of the mouth or hands or body which might not express the feeling of the song. They made the words clear in such a way that one could hear even the last syllable of every word, which was never interrupted or suppressed by passages and other embellishments.[5]

The care that the ladies took in their use of florid ornamentation may have reflected their contact with one of the greatest singing teachers of the day, the Florentine Giulio Caccini, who was called to Ferrara in 1592 to instruct them in the restrained manner of ornamentation that he later championed in his pioneering volume of solo songs with continuo accompaniment, *Le nuove musiche* (Florence, 1602),[6] and the same care not to obscure the text is found in most of Monteverdi's settings, with extended ornamentation usually applied only to stressed syllables.

We can take Giustiniani's account as a general indication of the style of singing cultivated by virtuosi in the early seventeenth century. But it is unlikely that much, if any of the music of Monteverdi's 1610 volume was sung by women. Women were forbidden to sing in public churches, at least in mixed ensembles, though nuns singing in their own choirs might have been able to make use of some at least of Monteverdi's sacred concertos. And if the concertos were used as spiritual chamber music – a possibility that Monteverdi mentions on the title-page – then women might have sung them in that context. For the most part, though, we must assume that the soprano lines of the Vespers were sung either by castrati or by boys or by a mixture of the two types of voice. Certainly virtuoso castrati were prized at the Mantuan court and in the papal chapel.

Of course, not all singers were equally endowed with the natural flexibility of the glottis needed to articulate ornamentation at high speed, and more than one late Renaissance commentator drew a distinction between church and chamber musicians: the former cultivated volume at the expense of flexibility of voice and clarity of text, while the latter sang more quietly and were more expert in ornamentation and musical oratory.[7] From such comments it might seem that the more able singers were reserved for chamber singing, but the reality was more complicated. Several authors of treatises on ornamentation were themselves church singers; in Rome the most able singers of the papal choir seem to have moved easily between church and chamber music; and at Mantua, if we agree with Graham Dixon's argument that much of the music of Monteverdi's 1610 volume was written for the patronal festival at Santa Barbara, it is reasonable to suppose that the choir of the chapel was augmented for that occasion by the best of the male court singers.

'Duo Seraphim'

Although the motets are arranged in Monteverdi's print in order of the number of voices required, ranging from 1 ('Nigra sum') to 6 ('Audi cœlum'), 'Duo Seraphim', for three tenors, is worth considering first. With its well-defined melodic structures and regular harmonic rhythm, it is perhaps the most approachable of the motets. It is also the most magnificent, and its opening paragraph, culminating in an exquisite sequence of dissonances depicting the seraphs' call resounding through the heavens, is one of the most memorable moments in the Vespers. It demands a considerable degree of virtuosity: Monteverdi's intention seems to have been to characterise the song of angels by using a style that represented the height of the singer's art in the early seventeenth century. He used a similarly florid style for the singing of Orpheus, the demigod of song, in the great Act III aria 'Possente spirto' of his opera *Orfeo* (1607); and later, in a letter of 9 December 1616, he actually stated that he liked in theatrical music to hear supernatural beings singing in an ornate style.[8]

The ornamental patterns that Monteverdi uses in bars 8–18 (Bt & St 15–28) and 35–56 (Bt & St 53–4) of 'Duo Seraphim' are very similar to those of 'Possente spirto', and may indicate that 'Duo Seraphim' was written at about the same time as or slightly later than the opera, though many of the figures that Monteverdi uses here and in the other motets and psalm settings can also be found in late sixteenth- and early seventeenth-century ornamentation manuals and other sources. The accelerating *passaggio* in bar 35 (Bt & St 53) of 'Duo Seraphim' and bar 7 (Bt 14; St 12) of 'Audi cœlum', for example, can also be found in bar 9 of 'Dalle più alte sfere' in the first *intermedio* for the play *La pellegrina* performed at Florence in 1589.[9] The trill on a single note at the end of bar 9 (Bt & St 18) appears in several late sixteenth-century treatises, as well as in the preface to Caccini's *Le nuove musiche*. The rising sequence of a quaver and two semiquavers that Monteverdi uses at the beginning of bar 9 (Bt & St 17) of 'Duo Seraphim' (and also in the psalm 'Lætatus sum' (bars 30–1 (Bt 57–8))) and in the 'Sonata sopra Sancta Maria' (bar 43 (Bt & St 83–4))) is a figure that Giovanni Battista Bovicelli suggests for ornamenting the interval of a rising second and Giovanni Luca Conforto as a pattern for filling in a rising fifth.[10] The devices that they suggest also include dotted patterns for scale passages (see Exx. 4(a) and (b)), though only Caccini seems to use these as an ornament for a single pitch, which he calls 'ribattuta di gola' (Ex. 4(c)).

The texts of motets could be chosen, shaped, or even specially written with musical setting in mind, unlike strictly liturgical texts, which had to be set in their entirety however unwieldy they might be from a composer's point of view. Nevertheless, three of the four motet texts set by Monteverdi have roots in the liturgy. The text of 'Duo Seraphim', for example, originated as a responsory compiled by Pope Innocent III (1198–1216)[11] from two biblical sources, Isaiah and the First Epistle of John. The responsory first appeared *c.* 1230 in breviaries of the Franciscan order, in which it was appointed to be sung from the Octave of the Epiphany until Septuagesima, and from the

Ex. 4(a) Bovicelli

Ex. 4(b) Conforto

Ex. 4(c) Caccini

first Sunday after Pentecost until Advent. In the Tridentine rite it appears as the eighth responsory at Matins on Trinity Sunday. The motet text, responsory and biblical texts are shown in Table 4.1 for comparison.

Despite its liturgical origins, the text offers various opportunities for musical metaphor. The most obvious of these is the juxtaposition of the phrases 'Duo Seraphim', 'Tres sunt' and 'Et hi tres unum sunt'. The first of these Monteverdi depicts by beginning the motet in the traditional way with two voices. At bar 31 (Bt & St 46) he introduces a third voice for 'Tres sunt'; and at bars 41–5 (Bt & St 61–8) he contrasts a three-note chord for 'Et hi tres' with a unison for 'unum sunt'.

There are other levels, too, at which the text offers opportunities for musical translation. The narrative of line 1 is contrasted with direct speech in lines 2–3, inviting a corresponding contrast of musical styles. Monteverdi responds by ending the narrative above a static bass at bars 8–10 (Bt & St 15–19), and then providing a simple melodic line dressed with ornamentation for the direct speech in bars 10–17 (Bt & St 20–9). He also dramatises the threefold statement 'Sanctus, sanctus, sanctus' by setting the word for each tenor in turn, before drawing the two voices into closer imitation for the last statement; at bars 45–56 (Bt & St 69–81), the same procedure is extended to draw in the third voice.

As well as providing opportunities for musical metaphor, the text as set by Monteverdi also contains parallels which allow the composer to create a satisfying musical structure. Monteverdi invents three

Table 4.1

Motet text	Responsory text[12]	Biblical text[13]
Duo Seraphim clamabant alter ad alterum:	Duo Seraphim clamabant alter ad alterum:	*Isias [Isaiah]* (6,2) Seraphim stabant super illud: (6,3) Et clamabant alter ad alterum, & dicebant
Sanctus, sanctus, sanctus Dominus Deus Sabaoth. Plena est omnis terra gloria eius.	Sanctus, sanctus, sanctus Dominus Deus Sabaoth. Plena est omnis terra gloria eius.	Sanctus, sanctus, sanctus, Dominus Deus exercituum, plena est omnis terra gloria eius.
Tres sunt qui testimonium dant in cœlo Pater, Verbum, et Spiritus Sanctus. Et hi tres unum sunt.	*V* Tres sunt qui testimonium dant in cœlo. Pater, Verbum, et Spiritus Sanctus. Et hi tres unum sunt.	*Epistula Iohannis 1 [First Epistle of John]* (5, 7) Quoniam tres sunt, qui testimonium dant in cælo: Pater, verbum, & spiritus sanctus: & hi tres unum sunt.
Sanctus, sanctus, sanctus Dominus Deus Sabaoth. Plena est omnis terra gloria eius.	Sanctus, sanctus, sanctus Dominus Deus Sabaoth.	*Isias [Isaiah]* (6,3) Sanctus, sanctus, sanctus, Dominus Deus exercituum plena est omnis terra gloria eius.
	Gloria Patri et Filio, et Spiritui Sancto. Plena est omnis terra gloria eius.	

discrete sections of material for the first three lines of the text: A (bars 1–10 (Bt & St 1–19)), B (10–21 (Bt & St 20–33)), C (21–30 (Bt & St 34–45)). When he brings in the third voice at 'Tres sunt' he builds an extended paragraph, using a declamatory style analogous to section A (bars 31–45 (Bt & St 46–68)), with a parenthetical threefold statement for 'Pater, Verbum, et Spiritus Sanctus', before repeating and developing the material of sections B (45–59 (Bt & St 69–84)) and C (59–70 (Bt & St 84–96)).

The melodic and harmonic language of 'Duo Seraphim' (and the other settings in the 1610 print) is modal. Cadence centres are not determined by tonal argument, but chosen from a range considered proper to (or permitted within) the mode and disposed to match the syntax and meaning of the text.[14] The mode of this motet is Mode 2, transposed to begin on G instead of D, necessitating a signature of one flat to maintain the intervallic structure of the mode.[15] The cadences that Monteverdi uses are restricted to G and D – defined by Pietro Pontio as the 'principal and final' cadence centres of transposed Mode 2 – with brief excursions to B flat for 'Dominus Deus Sabaoth' (bars 21 and 59 (Bt & St 33 and 84)), which Pontio describes as a 'quasi principal' cadence of the mode.[16]

As we have already noted, the text of 'Duo Seraphim' is not obviously linked to Marian devotion, though its Trinitarian associations would certainly have been appropriate for the feast of St Barbara who was martyred for her belief in the Trinity. It may be that Monteverdi included it in his publication either because he was particularly proud of the setting or because pressure of time meant that he had to include pieces that he had to hand whether entirely appropriate or not. But it may be unnecessarily idealistic to assume that late Renaissance choirmasters would have included in Vespers only motets that were absolutely germane to the feast being celebrated, especially if the motets did not function as antiphon-substitutes.

'Nigra sum' and 'Pulchra es'

The remaining motet texts are more clearly Marian in content, either through specific mention of her name, or by well-established association. The texts of 'Nigra sum' and 'Pulchra es', both drawn from the Song of Songs, fall into this latter category. The Song of Songs, or the

Table 4.2

Motet text	Liturgical text	Biblical text
		Canticum Canticorum Salomonis [*Song of Songs/Song of Solomon*]
Nigra sum sed formosa filiæ Ierusalem. Ideo dilexit me Rex et introduxit in cubiculum suum et dixit mihi:	*Third antiphon of Second Vespers of the Common of Feasts of the Blessed Virgin* Nigra sum sed formosa, filiæ Ierusalem: ideo dilexit me rex, et introduxit me in cubiculum suum.	(1,5) Nigra sum, sed formosa, filiae Ierusalem (1,4) Introduxit me rex in cellaria sua: (2,10) En dilectus meus loquitur mihi:
surge, amica mea, et veni	*Fourth antiphon of Second Vespers of the Common of Feasts of the Blessed Virgin*	(2,10) Surge, propera amica mea, columba mea, formosa mea, & veni.
iam hiems transiit imber abiit et recessit	Jam hiems transiit, imber abiit et recessit: surge amica mea, et veni	(2,11) Iam enim hiems transiit, imber abiit, & recessit
flores apparuerunt in terra nostra tempus putationis advenit.		(2,12) Flores apparuerunt in terra nostra, tempus putationis advenit:

Table 4.3

Motet text	Liturgical text	Biblical text
		Canticum Canticorum Salomonis [*Song of Songs/Song of Solomon*]
Pulchra es amica mea suavis et decora filia Ierusalem Pulchra es amica mea suavis et decora sicut Ierusalem	*Fifth Antiphon of Second Vespers for the Feast of the Assumption of the Blessed Virgin* Pulchra es et decora, filia Ierusalem:	(6,3) Pulchra es amica mea, suavis, & decora sicut Ierusalem: terribilis ut castrorum acies ordinata.
terribilis ut castrorum acies ordinata. Averte oculos tuos a me quia ipsi me avolare fecerunt.	terribilis ut castrorum acies ordinata.	(6,4) Averte oculos tuos a me, quia ipsi me avolare fecerunt.

Song of Solomon as it is known in the English translation of the Bible, is an anthology of love lyrics whose acceptance among the canonical books of scripture in both Jewish and Christian traditions seems to have depended on its being interpreted as an allegory. In the Jewish and Christian traditions respectively, the Song has been interpreted as depicting the Lord's relationship with Israel and Christ's relationship with his church. From the Middle Ages onwards, however, it was customary to identify the 'beloved' of the Song, who speaks in 'Nigra sum' and is addressed in 'Pulchra es', as the Virgin Mary, and texts from the Song were admitted as part of the Marian liturgy, as, for example, in the fifth antiphon for the Feast of the Assumption (see Appendix 1). The first line of 'Nigra sum' – 'I am black, but beautiful' – may seem puzzling at first, but the biblical context makes it clear that the maiden is sunburned from working in the vineyard, rather than literally 'black'; her complexion does not match the urban notion of beauty, hence her need to justify it.[17] (A more literal interpretation of the line has led to the veneration of black Madonnas in various parts of Europe.)

The two Song of Songs texts that Monteverdi set are a mixture of biblical texts and the versions of those texts used as Vespers antiphons in the *Antiphonale*. In the case of 'Nigra sum' the relationship between the texts is quite complex (see Table 4.2).

The first two lines of Monteverdi's text are quite clearly based on the Vespers antiphon, since the antiphon reverses the order of the lines and other details of the biblical text. The additional 'et dixit mihi', however, restores the essence, if not the actual words, of the Bible in order to lead naturally from narrative to direct speech. The passage of direct speech itself – 'surge amica mea ... tempus putationis advenit' – follows the order of the biblical text, though the omission of the words 'propera', 'columba mea' and 'formosa mea' suggests contamination by the associated antiphon.

Similarly, 'Pulchra es' begins as though it were the antiphon text, but this is then 'corrected' and filled out by reference to the biblical original (see Table 4.3).

It is, perhaps, worth emphasising that although these texts are related to Vespers antiphons, their compilers took them outside the bounds of the liturgy by adding to, and reordering them.

'Nigra sum' and 'Pulchra es' form a pair in other respects, too.

Since both are essentially love-songs Monteverdi sets them in styles virtually indistinguishable from those of contemporary secular songs of the same kind. Both are set in Mode 8, confirmed by Monteverdi's use of prominent cadences on C ('Nigra sum', bars 10, 12 and 13 (Bt 20, 23, 26; St 20, 23, 25); 'Pulchra es', bars 21 and 23 (Bt 34, 37; St 28, 30));[18] both have exactly the same ambitus in relation to the final; both are cast in ABB' form; and both make use of ornamentation seemingly derived from the work of Caccini: in particular the dotted figures (see, for example, 'Nigra sum', end of bar 3 (Bt & St 6); 'Pulchra es', bars 1–23 (Bt 15–37; St 12–30) *passim*) that Caccini recommends as having 'more grace' than plain quaver patterns.[19]

Monteverdi's choice of voices for these two motets may seem perverse by modern standards. 'Nigra sum', a text in which the maiden reports the words of her beloved, is set for solo tenor,[20] while 'Pulchra es', the words of the male lover, is set for two sopranos. We should remember, however, that Monteverdi was writing for the Church and would assume that only male singers were available to him. He may have chosen the tenor voice for 'Nigra sum' because its darker colour matched the image of blackness in the first line. And the choice of high voices for 'Pulchra es', words uttered by the king, may be related to the idea that high voices were associated with superiority in a hierarchical society.[21] At all events, there are also many examples in early seventeenth-century secular music of songs in which female emotions are portrayed by male voices and vice versa.

Monteverdi's setting of 'Nigra sum' owes a great deal in its conception to the type of continuo-accompanied solo song pioneered by Caccini and promoted through *Le nuove musiche*. In his songs Caccini pioneered the use of a skeleton harmonic outline (basso continuo) rather than the fully written-out contrapuntal accompaniment that had been the norm in sixteenth-century solo song. His aim was to allow the singer greater freedom to declaim the vocal line rhetorically and thus to move the passions of the audience, and the techniques that he recommended to the singer in the preface to the book – rubato, crescendo and decrescendo, 'esclamazioni', a limited use of ornamentation – were also designed to project the rhetoric of his songs.

The study of rhetoric – the art of the orator to persuade and move the passions of an audience – formed part of the *trivium* of spoken arts in the Middle Ages and remained an important element of the educational process in the Renaissance. It provided a training for statesmen, lawyers and clergymen in the construction of an argument and its embellishment through the use of figures of speech, the simplest of which is repetition used to reinforce an important statement. Rhetorical modes of thought also inform the literature of the Renaissance and musical settings of literary texts, and at the beginning of the seventeenth century German theorists in particular began to codify musical devices that they identified as paralleling verbal figures of speech. Their attempts were not always consistent, as is shown by the list in George Buelow's *New Grove* article 'Rhetoric and Music'. Nevertheless, they provide us with a way of approaching the 'new music' of the early seventeenth century in general and a motet like 'Nigra sum' in particular.

'Nigra sum' is particularly interesting in that it illustrates two applications of rhetoric in music. In the B section of the motet (bars 14–28 (Bt 27–56; St 26–48)), in which the king's speech is reported, Monteverdi uses impassioned declamation of a kind found in his early operas. In the motet's A section, however, he uses rhetorical devices to argue two related propositions: (1) 'I am black, but beautiful, daughters of Jerusalem', and (2) 'therefore the king has loved me and brought me into his chamber'; it is possible to suggest a reading of this in rhetorical terms.

The opening phrase, 'Nigra sum' (I am black), is set low – that is, in a 'dark' area of the tenor's tessitura. This statement is followed by a silence (*abruptio* (No. 57 in the list in the *New Grove* 'Rhetoric and Music)), intended to highlight its importance. The next word, 'sed' ('but'), is set an octave higher and on a syncopated entry, emphasising the idea of contradiction; the leaping figure used (*antitheton* (48)) introduces the antithesis of blackness and beauty. Following this, the whole antithetical phrase 'but beautiful, O daughters' is stated, and repeated twice with varied music, omitting the word 'sed' on the first repetition and 'filiae' on the second so that the word 'formosa' (beautiful) is first emphasised by the high D, and then brought into focus at the cadence (bar 4 (Bt & St 7)).

The first line of text is then repeated and further intensified. Following the initial 'Nigra sum' (bars 4–5 (Bt & St 8–9)), this time emphasised by a syncopated beginning, and *abruptio*, the voice leaps, not an octave, but a ninth, emphasising the antithesis even more strongly; the following two phrases – 'sed formosa' and 'formosa filiae' – are set to identical pitches, but to varied rhythms (*paranomasia* (12)), and the line ends with an emphatic cadence on A.

There follows a musico-rhetorical device that has no counterpart in purely verbal rhetoric. By setting the word 'ideo' (therefore) at bar 8 (Bt & St 15) to identifiably the same musical phrase as 'Nigra sum', and then repeating it a fourth higher (*synonomia* (17)), Monteverdi makes the point that the king loves the maiden not in spite of, but because she is dark in colour – 'Nigra sum … ideo dilexit me Rex' (I am black … therefore the king has loved me). The positive nature of the statement is emphasised by the threefold use of a perfect cadence on C for 'dilexit me Rex' (bar 10 (Bt & St 20)), 'et introduxit in cubiculum suum' (bar 12 (Bt & St 23)) and 'et dixit mihi' (bar 13 (Bt 26; St 25)); all three statements are thereby conceptually prefaced by the word 'ideo' which was sung on the pitch C at bar 9.

The B section – the king's reported speech – begins with an obvious madrigalism, as the word 'surge' (arise) is set to a rising scale passage (*anabasis* (39)) spanning the full ambitus of the piece before cadencing on D. More subtly, the accompanying bass pattern which begins as though in strict imitation of the voice, is further 'raised' chromatically through F sharp and G sharp. After a shortened repeat of the scale motif, cadencing on G (bar 17 (Bt 34; St 32)), Monteverdi invents a new, more persuasive and more urgent rising pattern for the complete phrase 'surge … et veni', pressing on through it to take in the next two lines of text before cadencing on D at bar 23 (Bt 46; St 44). At the height of the line, the last 'veni' arrives at the note F, creating a powerful dissonance with the bass, which has not yet reached the intended harmony note of D. The twofold sense of poignancy and urgency that this type of exclamation suggests is a device familiar from Monteverdi's operatic language: he uses a similar device at the beginning of the *Lamento d'Arianna* and at various points in the score of *Orfeo* – at the end of the duet of mourning 'Chi ne consola, ahi lassi?' in Act II (Malipiero edn, p. 70, bar 5) and in Orpheus's Act V lament (Malipiero edn, p. 140, bar 9).

After this, the setting that Monteverdi chooses for 'tempus putationis' (the time of pruning) – a series of semibreves on a monotone D – seems rather puzzling. What is intended by the musical image? Should the line be sung plain or ornamented? A possible answer is that the intended image is that of a bell, symbolising time ('tempus') and also suggesting rejoicing, a musical image that had been used in musical settings since the fifteenth century.[22] When this passage is heard again in shortened note values at the end of the repeated B section, the new crotchet bass, falling in a scale passage, also suggests a peal of bells. If this interpretation is correct, then it would be inappropriate to obscure the image by ornamenting the vocal line.

Where 'Nigra sum' begins in a declamatory style, the A section of 'Pulchra es' is lyrical, while the B and B' sections (bars 23–43 (Bt 38–64; St 31–56) and 43–60 (Bt 64–91; St 56–81) respectively) present a mixture of declamation and lyricism. The initial line of text, the whole of which is restated and varied when the second voice enters, is unusually long: too long, in fact, to be taken in one melodic phrase. Monteverdi deftly overcomes this problem by dividing the line into syntactical sub-units – 'Pulchra es amica mea', 'suavis et decora', 'filia Jerusalem' – ending each in a way which implies continuity between them: after 'mea' the move to the bass G produces a strong dissonance with the vocal line which propels it on to the word 'suavis', and after the cadence on 'decora' the bass moves on in crotchets towards the word 'filia'. When the second voice enters we can see that the apparently bizarre decision to include in the text both the version of line 1 from the antiphon and its original form from the Vulgate in fact has a logic in that it provides a rationale for varying the ending of the line musically.

At bar 24 there is a sudden change from a C major cadence to an E major harmony, providing a musical image for the text 'averte' (turn away), and the texture changes to solo declamation, complete with a rhetorical repetition figure for the phrase 'a me' (*climax* or *auxesis* (4)), leading to a triple-metre setting of 'me avolare fecerunt' with word repetition as if in a small-scale aria. There is a question mark over the meaning of Monteverdi's use of triple metre in this context. Most performers, perhaps assuming that it is a metaphor for 'flee away', take it at a fast tempo, making the proportion between it and the preceding section o· in triple metre = ♩ of the preceding duple. However, Roger Bowers has argued that the correct proportion here is o· = o, which produces a much slower triple metre, and one that hardly illustrates 'flee away' literally. The effect is, rather, one of languorous pleasure. The phrases that follow offer some support to this interpretation.

When the music changes back to duple metre at bar 35 (Bt 54, St 46), the dotted rhythms do, indeed, suggest a metaphor for fleeing; but at bar 39 (Bt 58; St 50) this gives way to a highly charged line with powerful dissonances between bass and voice (including C sharp against C natural in bar 40 (Bt 59; St 51)). Here Monteverdi seems not to be translating the words literally, but to be suggesting the powerful emotion produced by the beloved's eyes. (This interpretation is conveyed very convincingly on The Scholars' 1995 recording.)

'Audi cœlum'

'Nigra sum' and 'Pulchra es' might as easily have been written as chamber music as for church use. The more restrained and leisurely recitative style of 'Audi cœlum', however, seems designed for a larger space and to owe less to Caccini and to Monteverdi's experience as an opera composer. The long winding *passaggi* of bars 25–7 and 46–7 (Bt 40–4 and 82–3; St 37–41 and 71–2), and the disruption of consecutive syllables of the text by ornaments in bars 14–17 (Bt 25–8; St 22–5) seem to belong to an older, or at least a different tradition.[23]

The text is a Marian devotion cast in the form of eight apparently freely invented stanzas[24] each followed by an echo, and a final line reminiscent of various Marian liturgical texts. The use of an echo, in which the last syllables of the stanza are repeated, or truncated in order to form a different word in answer, had been established in Italian music for well over a century before the publication of the Vespers, particularly in secular and theatrical music.[25] In the case of 'Audi cœlum' the echo is a voice from the heavens which responds first to a stanza of invocation, then to five stanzas of questions, to which it provides the answers, and finally in response to two stanzas of exhortation.

Monteverdi's setting is somewhat experimental in form. Instead of composing the whole motet for two voices, he responds to the word 'Omnes' (all) in stanza 7 (bars 45ff. (Bt 80ff.; St 69ff.)) by introducing an ensemble of six voices from which the solo and echo emerge at the end of the stanza; this process is repeated with almost exactly the same music for stanza 8 (bars 70ff. (Bt 128ff.; St 117ff.)), though with new music for the echo, which ends with a typically Caccinian ornament

for the words 'solamen ... amen'. The final line of the motet is again
set for six voices.

The use of soloists set against an ensemble refrain was one that
Monteverdi had already successfully employed in his madrigal 'Ahi,
come a un vago sol' (fifth book of madrigals, 1605). In 'Audi cœlum',
however, the ensemble is grafted uncomfortably on to the end of the
motet rather than forming an integral part of the conception, and the
sense of unease is increased by the fact that performers usually increase the tempo at this point so that the triple-metre passages will not
be too slow; some performers actually double time at bar 48 (Bt 85; St
74), so that the rhythm of that bar appears exactly the same as the
dotted minim and crotchet at the end of bar 47 (Bt 84; St 73). It is
tempting to speculate that Monteverdi may have rewritten what was
originally a motet for two voices only in order to produce a more
'interesting' piece for his 1610 publication.

'Audi cœlum' is written in an untransposed Mode 1, though its
ambitus extends a full fourth below what one would normally expect.
The extension to A is, however, used only twice, in bars 16 and 27 (Bt
27 and 43; St 24 and 40), in both cases in order to provide long
ascending lines painting the rising of the dawn and the word 'heavens'
respectively. The majority of cadences are on the principal pitches D
and A, with use of what Pontio calls the 'quasi principal' centre of F at
bar 10 at the point where the text moves from invocation to question-
ing. Interestingly, the last full cadence of the motet on to D, the final
of the mode, occurs at bar 100 (Bt 185; St 170), five bars before the end
of the motet, leaving the voices to circle round a series of plagal
cadences in an apt image for the eternity of 'in seculorum secula'.

During the course of the motet there are, however, several cadences
on C, a centre which Pontio defines as 'not proper' to the mode and to
be used only 'in passing, and with care'.[26] Some of these cadences are,
however, quite prominent, particularly those at bars 38, 41 and 44 (Bt
65, 71 and 77; St 56, 61 and 66), and the last two are underlined by a
rhetorically emphatic repetition of the melodic line of stanza 5 ('Illa
sacra et fœlix porta ...', bars 39–41 (Bt 67–72; St 58–62)) for the words
of stanza 6 ('Quæ semper tutum ...', bars 42–4 (Bt 73–7; St 63–7)).
The references here are to Mary as the gateway through which eternal
life entered the world. Monteverdi seems to be using an unexpected

cadence centre to underline the doctrinal importance of this passage –
Mary's fulfilment of Ezekiel's prophecy. The biblical passage in question is Ezekiel 44:2, describing the eastern gate of the temple: 'Then
said the Lord unto me; This gate shall be shut, it shall not be opened,
and no man shall enter in by it; Because the Lord, the God of Israel,
hath entered in by it, therefore it shall be shut.' This was interpreted
by St Jerome as referring to Mary, the door through which Christ
entered the world,[27] a door which was thus closed to humans. The
phrase 'the closed door' was regularly used during the Middle Ages as
one of the names of Mary.[28]

'Sonata sopra Sancta Maria'

The 'Sonata sopra Sancta Maria', scored for soprano, eight instruments (two violins, two cornetti, three trombones, the second of which
may be substituted by a *viuola da brazzo*, and one other *viuola*) and
continuo, was the first item of the Vespers to be published in the
present century, and it is easy to understand why editors were at-
tracted to this, one of the grandest and most brilliant pieces in the
collection. In the early seventeenth century, too, the sudden appearance of a vocal *cantus firmus* in an ostensibly instrumental piece must
have provoked surprise and delight, for only one other similar work
had appeared in print, in the *Primo libro de' concerti ecclesiastici* (1608)
of the Ferrarese monk Archangelo Crotti.[29] The sonata has been considered one of the most Venetian works in Monteverdi's collection,
because of its obvious similarity to the canzonas and sonatas of Giovanni Gabrieli. However, as Kurtzman has pointed out, the relationship is only a superficial one.[30]

According to David Blazey,[31] the *cantus firmus* is a variant of a
plainsong phrase taken from the Litany of the Saints, though its intervallic structure is actually rather closer to the appropriate phrase in the
Cantus Litanarium given in Guidetti's *Directorium Chori*, which has a
one-flat signature (see Appendix 2, p. 116). In the context of the
sonata the eleven statements of the plainsong themselves form a sort of
litany (a series of petitions). As Table 4.4 shows, the Sonata is a
ternary structure.

The A section consists of an initial idea, its transformation into

Table 4.4

Section	Bar nos.	Metre	*Cantus firmus*	Motif(s)
A	1–8 (Bt & St 1–16)	¢	—	A, B
	9–17 (Bt & St 17–32)	3/2	—	A, B
	17–19 (Bt & St 32–6)	¢	—	—
B	19–40 (Bt & St 36–78)	¢	1	B, A, C
	40–51 (Bt & St 78–99)	¢	2	A and inversion
	51–8 (Bt & St 99–113)	¢ → 3/2	3	A
	58–70 (Bt & St 112–30)	3/2 & ¢	4	A inverted
	70–82 (Bt 130–54; St 130–42)	3/2	5	C
	82–97 (Bt 154–85; St 142–72)	3/2	6	B
	97–105 (Bt 185–200; St 173–88)	3/2	7	C
	105–16 (Bt 200–22; St 188–210)	3/2	8	C
	115–34 (Bt 221–59; St 209–47)	3/2	9	C inverted
A'	135–42 (Bt 260–75; St 248–63)	¢	—	A, B
	143–51 (Bt 276–91; St 264–79)	3/2	10	A, B
	151–4 (Bt 291–7; St 279–85)	¢	11	—

triple metre, and a short coda. This is followed by nine statements of the *cantus firmus* accompanied by various (but not always entirely discrete) instrumental textures; in the last of these statements the *cantus firmus* is broken into short, sobbing phrases. In the final section the initial idea is again stated instrumentally, but the triple-metre variant and coda prove to be yet further accompaniments to the *cantus firmus*. The B section of the sonata mirrors the division of the introduction into duple- and triple-metre sections.

The sonata gives the impression of a wealth of thematic ideas. However, a closer examination shows that there are really only three basic motifs which are varied by being clothed with different ornamental figures and, sometimes, inverted. The opening encapsulates two of these motifs – motif A is a scale descending through the interval of a fifth; motif B is a sequence of two falling thirds separated by a rising second (Ex. 5). The two motifs are separated out in the passage which introduces the first statement of the *cantus firmus*. Motif B is stated in long note values at bars 19–21 (Bt & St 37–40) (Ex. 6(a)) and contrasted at bar 24 (Bt & St 45) with a passage of lively dotted rhythms decorating overlapping statements of motif A (Ex. 7). At bar 26 (Bt & St 49) a third motif, C, is introduced, consisting of a sequence

Ex. 5

Ex. 6

San - cta   Ma - ri - a

Ex. 7

Ex. 8(a)

Ex. 8(b)

Ex. 8(c)

Ex. 8(d)

of rising fourths separated by falling thirds (Ex. 8(a)). (Motif B, which appears to be freely invented, proves to be the bass used to harmonise the opening of the first *cantus firmus* statement (Ex. 6(b)).

All three motifs are subjected to various transformations. At bar 42 (Bt & St 81), for example, motif A is combined heterophonically with another version of itself, in Cornetto I and Trombone II (Ex. 9), and then presented in inversion a bar later. And at bar 82 (Bt 154; St 142) motif B is turned into a lilting triple-metre melody. Most of the motivic usage is readily identifiable and is shown in Table 4.4. The material used for statement 5 of the *cantus firmus*, and then developed for statements 7 and 9, appears new but is, in fact, derived from the intervals of C (by inversion in the last case); see Exx. 8b–d respectively.

The first motets with continuo had appeared in 1602 in the *Cento concerti ecclesiastici* of Monteverdi's Mantuan contemporary Lodovico Viadana. Considering how few other collections of continuo motets appeared in the first decade of the century, the sacred concertos of the 1610 publication appear remarkably inventive and mature. Paradoxically, one of the reasons for this is that Monteverdi was first and foremost a composer of secular and theatrical music: the technical difficulty of 'Duo Seraphim' and the use of the new styles of solo song and opera reflect his experience in working with the best chamber singers and instrumentalists of his day. The motets and the 'Sonata sopra Sancta Maria' are, in short, pieces at the forefront of stylistic developments in the first decade of the seventeenth century.

5

'And all on a cantus firmus*'*

Whether prompted by Mantuan precedent or an eye to papal reception, Monteverdi's decision to set the strictly liturgical texts of the Vespers service on appropriate plainsong *cantus firmi* was a strategy that had several advantages. It enabled him to present himself as a composer competent to work with the basic musical language of the Church and to demonstrate the range of invention that he could bring to *cantus firmus* based pieces. It allowed him to show that such settings, though conservative at base, could incorporate thoroughly up-to-date elements of musical style. And, perhaps not least, it helped him solve a problem inherent in setting the psalms and Magnificat – that of achieving musical coherence when working with texts that were sometimes long and unwieldy and certainly not designed for setting by an early seventeenth-century madrigalist.

The texts that Monteverdi set and the plainsongs he used are shown in Appendix 2 and, in the case of the psalms and Magnificat settings, the parts bearing the psalm tones are identified. Monteverdi uses not only the pitches of the plainsongs as the basis of his settings, but also their verse and/or phrase structures, so that his settings appear, as I suggested earlier, rather like *falsobordone* settings projected on to a larger canvas. For this reason the logic of the settings is most easily followed if the texts are laid out with the verse divisions found in the original liturgical books, as shown in Appendix 2 (in this scheme the doxology – the 'Gloria Patri ...' – sung at the end of each psalm and the Magnificat forms the last two verses of each setting and has been numbered accordingly). In all but one of the psalm settings and the Magnificats Monteverdi parodies the liturgical practice of having a cantor or cantors begin the psalm before the choir joins in. The exception is 'Nisi Dominus', whose initial ten-part texture may well have been suggested by considerations of word-painting; even here, though, the texture of the first verse sets it off from the schematic chanting that follows.

Response 'Domine ad adiuvandum'

'Sex vocib[us] & sex Instrumentis, si placet' (i.e. the instruments may be omitted and the response chanted as *falsobordone*). The rubric's reference to six instruments means only that there are six instrumental lines; the part-books actually call for twelve instruments and continuo: two cornetts, three trombones, two *violini da brazzo*, four *viuole da brazzo* and one *contrabasso da gamba*.

The response which opens the Vespers is a piece whose brilliance is matched only by the audacity of its conception. If it is based on a plainsong at all, then that plainsong is probably the version of 'Deus in adiutorium–Domine ad adiuvandum' set for double and semi-double feasts in Guidetti's *Directorium Chori* (p. 510). However, as we can see from Appendix 2, p. 105, Monteverdi has reduced even this to its reciting note alone, sung without even the simple cadential formulae of the original. He did this in order to reuse the instrumental 'toccata' that had prefaced his opera *Orfeo*. Just as in *Orfeo* the music of the Toccata is sounded three times, the three statements encompassing, respectively, the response and the two sentences of the doxology. Each statement is separated from the next by a passage in triple metre for the instruments alone, the music of which is then slightly adapted for the final Alleluia. By reusing such clearly recognisable material from *Orfeo* Monteverdi also lent a subtext to the response: the music that had been a call-to-attention for a notable Gonzaga entertainment now provides a call-to-attention at the beginning of Vespers, but the implied compliment to the Gonzagas remains, and would also have been evident to anyone outside Mantua who had studied the score of *Orfeo*, published at Venice in 1609.

We can assume that the Vespers version is later than the Toccata not only because it has voices added, but also because the instrumental accompaniment is itself a more complex reworking of the original. Where the Toccata was scored for five instruments, the response is scored for six: the second cornetto/*violino da brazzo* part, which plays in canon and in harmony with the first, has been added, and other small modifications made. We do not, for example, hear the complete material of the Toccata each time. The first statement extends to only eight bars. These are reused and ornamented for 'Gloria Patri ... Spiritui Sancto' and extended to take in an extra bar of the original (bars 14–22; Bt 16–24). The full version of the remodelled Toccata is reserved for 'Sicut erat in principio ... Amen' (bars 28–43; Bt 32–47).

'Dixit Dominus'

'Sex vocib[us] & sex Instrumentis. Li Ritornelli si ponno sonare & anco tralasciar secondo il volere' (the instrumental ritornelli may be omitted). The instrumentation of the ritornelli is not specified. The setting is in Mode 4, untransposed. Most cadences are on A, and Monteverdi sharpens all but the last G of the tone to reinforce the sense of this tonal centre. Endings on E, the other principal cadence centre of the mode, are approached irregularly and tend to involve false relations between the G of the psalm tone and the G sharp of the *tierce de Picardie*, as at bar 11 (Bt 21–2). The intonation of the psalm tone is used in verse 1 only, and the tone is sung untransposed in verses 1, 3, 5 and 7. The doxology is particularly interesting from the point of view of tonal manipulation. Monteverdi's decision to transpose the psalm tone to begin on G at bar 114 (Bt 214), with a G minor harmony that stands well outside the norms of Mode 4, is startling. But transposing to begin on G means that the tone then ends on D, so that Monteverdi can comfortably begin the next verse with the tone transposed to begin on D (bar 121 Bassus (Bt 228)). That transposition ends on A (bar 134 Cantus (Bt 255)), allowing Monteverdi to round off the setting with a plagal cadence on to E, the final of the mode. Presumably, then, his decision to begin the doxology on G was arrived at by a process of reverse planning; its outcome, however, is one of the most striking moments in the 1610 Vespers.

As befits the first of the psalm settings in the collection, 'Dixit Dominus' demonstrates Monteverdi's acquaintance with two standard methods of singing the psalms in polyphony: through adding counterpoints above or around a plain (though rhythmicised) *cantus firmus* (the *intonatio* of the psalm tone is omitted after verse 1), and by using *falsobordone*. Monteverdi alternates these two types of setting, verse by verse, in an essentially schematic manner (see Table 5.1) which parallels the pattern used in simpler services of alternating plainsong and

Table 5.1

Verse	Incipit	Technique	Scoring	Initial pitch of psalm tone
1	Dixit Dominus	solo intonation merging into six-part counterpoint	6vv	A
2	Donec ponam	*falsobordone*	6vv	
3	Virgam virtutis	*cantus firmus* with counterpoint	S, then SSB	A
4	Tecum principium	*falsobordone*	6vv	
5	Iuravit dominus	*cantus firmus* with counterpoint	T, then TTB	A
6	Dominus a dextris	*falsobordone*	6vv	
7	Iudicabit in nationibus	*cantus firmus* with counterpoint	ATB, then full 6vv	A
8	De torrente in via	falsobordone	6vv	
9	Gloria Patri	solo intonation,	T	G
10	Sicut erat	followed by six-part counterpoint	6vv	D

falsobordone. Verse 1 and the doxology (verses 9 and 10) stand slightly apart from the main scheme.

In verse 1 Monteverdi parodies the idea of cantors initiating the psalm and the choir responding by presenting the first half of the psalm tone in imitation, together with a counter-subject; the second half of the verse – the point at which the choir would normally enter – is set for the full ensemble and, incidentally, matches the passage of direct speech. Verse 2 presents us with the first passage of *falsobordone*. The *falsobordone* setting is of the type without *cantus firmus*. Instead, Monteverdi uses a reciting chord of A minor for the first half-verse, and G major for the second. Each half-verse ends with an extended sequence based on a descending scale rounded off by a cadence; and the whole verse is followed by an optional ritornello. The material of the ritornello is based on the melodic sequence invented for the second half-verse. The same pattern is followed in verses 4, 6 and 8, with newly invented figuration for each of the sequences. The pattern set up in verse 2 of a triple-metre sequence at the end of the first half-verse and duple metre at the end of the second is broken at verses 6 and 8, though in the latter case the syncopated figuration implies a triple pattern. The expected ritornello between the end of verse 8 and the beginning of the doxology is omitted, so that there is a further element of surprise as the solo tenor intones the 'Gloria Patri'.

In each half of verses 3 and 5, the psalm tone is given out on the organ bass while a solo voice sings an ornamented counterpoint against it; then the Bassus sings the tone with the organ while two upper voices sing the counterpoint to it. Verse 7 provides an inventive climax to this pattern. Here, the first half-verse is begun by Bassus and Tenor, singing the psalm tone in parallel thirds, with the Altus following a semibreve later a fifth above the Bassus; in the full texture that follows, the parallel sounding out of the psalm tone is transferred to Cantus, Sextus and Bassus, while the inner voices fill in the texture with dotted rhythms. The pattern is repeated for the second half-verse except that the Altus initiates the psalm tone and is then followed by Tenor and bass in parallel, and that in the full section a new syncopated counterpoint is invented for the inner parts.

At first sight this pattern appears to be independent of the meaning of the text, but it is possible to see some levels at which texture and figuration may be metaphors for textual ideas. The psalm is about the power of a vengeful God, first mentioned in verse 2, which may have provided Monteverdi with the motive for using a full texture here. Similar sentiments of war and domination are expressed in verses 4 and 6, and the dotted rhythms used for the sequences in verse 6 may have been suggested by a long tradition in which whip and sword blows in particular, and battle in general, had been painted by the use of dotted rhythms.[1] The metaphor 'full texture = power' is not apt for verse 8, but Monteverdi actually manages to make this verse seem less forceful by contrast with the energy of verse 7, the climactic point of the second pattern.

'Laudate pueri'

'À 8 voci sole nel Organo.' The setting is in Mode 8, untransposed, with primary cadences on G, D and C (the median cadence of Psalm

Tone 8). The only other cadence centre used is A, which Pontio defines as a transitory cadence for this mode.[2] The psalm tone is presented with its intonation in verses 1 and 10, but begins on the reciting note in the other verses; minor adjustments are made to the termination formula in verses 3, 4 and 5. The psalm tone is transposed down a fourth in verses 2 and 3, which allows the introduction of cadences on D, and up a tone in verse 4, allowing a cadence on A.

There is some dispute as to whether this psalm should be scored for two choirs or simply as an eight-part texture with two of each voice-part. The only indication that Monteverdi might have intended double-choir setting is found in the second bass part (in the Septimus part-book), which has the rubric 'secundi chori'. Following this, Bartlett and Stevens score the psalm for two choirs. Roche rejects this, saying (p. xxiii) 'The only point where 2 groups of voices emerge is at "Gloria Patri" (89–102 [Bt 162–89; St 133–46]), and then they are in dialogue with the solo voice carrying the psalm tone rather than with each other.'

As in 'Dixit Dominus', the text is set verse by verse, though with a less formulaic series of textures, and here the psalm tone is heard in each verse. There is, however, an overlap between verses 3 and 4: the text of verse 3 is set in Cantus and Sextus at bars 21–5 (Bt 42–9; St 28–35), with only the first half of the psalm tone in the Altus; the Altus then continues with the second half of the tone while Tenor and Quintus sing the first half of verse 4. Only then is the whole psalm tone sung by the Cantus to the words of verse 4.

The reason for this is textual, for whereas in 'Dixit Dominus' the larger-scale organisation of the setting is created by abstract patterning, in 'Laudate pueri' Monteverdi groups the verses into larger units suggested by the meaning of the text. Thus, verses 1 to 3 are concerned with praising God, while 4 and 5 invite contemplation of the glory of a God who dwells high in the heavens. Verses 6 to 8 deal with God's interventions in human affairs. The doxology (verses 9 and 10) is a separate entity.

Monteverdi's setting follows this broad scheme, though he also draws the doxology into his overall plan by reusing the material from verse 1 for 'Sicut erat in principio', a procedure that wittily encapsulates the meaning of the text – 'As it was in the beginning, is now and ever shall be' – and he caps this by letting the Amen, which begins for six voices, trail off seemingly endlessly in a duet for two tenors. As in 'Dixit Dominus' he also sets verse 1 apart from those that follow by creating an imitative texture based on the psalm tone, for each half of which he creates a counter-subject. *Pace* Roche, there is a certain amount of interplay between choirs in this verse. After the initial solo statement of the first half of the psalm tone, tone and counter-subject are presented first by Altus and Tenor of Choir 1, then by Septimus and Quintus – the alto and tenor of Choir 2 – before the texture builds towards a final eight-voice texture with the tone in the soprano of Choir 1 and the counter-subject in the bass of Choir 2. A similar procedure is used for the second half of the tone.

Verse 1 and the 'Sicut erat', then, establish a frame for the setting. Verses 2 to 5 are set as a series of duets for two voices of equal range, accompanying the psalm tone in a third voice. There is a certain amount of simple word-painting – rising patterns for 'excelsus' (high) and 'et super cœlos' (and above the heavens) in verse 4, for example (bars 25 and 27–8 (Bt 49–50 & 53–5; St 35–6 & 39–41)). More importantly, though, Monteverdi is here setting up the basis of an elaborate musical conceit. By analogy with the usage in 'Duo Seraphim', the ornamented style of the duets may be taken as representing seventeenth-century singers exercising their artistry in praise of God. This idea is set up in verse 2 and continued to the end of verse 5. In the setting of verse 2 and the first half of verse 3 (bars 14–25 (Bt 28–49; St 14–35)) the psalm tone is always heard in the lowest of the three voices. The transition from verse 3 to verse 4 is an important juncture. At bar 25 (Bt 49; St 35), where verses 3 and 4 overlap, the psalm tone emerges at the top of the texture, above the words 'Excelsus super omnes gentes dominus' (The Lord is high above all nations). For the remainder of verses 4 and 5 the psalm tone soars, usually an octave or more above its accompanying duets, representing God high above the mortals singing his praises.

Thus far this may seem little more than literal, even naïve, word-painting. However, having established the idea of the psalm tone as a personification – of God in this case – Monteverdi is able to carry the idea forward into his setting of verses 6 to 8, where God intervenes in the affairs of men and women. After a transition (bars 43–9 (Bt 78–88; St 64–74)) in which two basses paint the idea of the descent from heaven to earth, all parts except the Altus sing 'Suscitans a terra' (He raiseth up [the poor] out of the dust). Monteverdi's ascending line is an obvious musical image for the raising, but his use of triple metre is also a well-established metaphor for pleasure. The Latin word-order, which places 'inopem' (literally 'the destitute') at the end of the phrase, allows Monteverdi to omit it from the images of raising and pleasure, so that it is heard only in the much thinner – and therefore 'poorer' – duple-metre texture that follows (bars 52–5 (Bt 93–8; St 77–82)) in which the psalm tone is given to the Altus at the top of the texture. At bar 56 (Bt 99; St 82) the psalm tone ceases before it has run its full course as Monteverdi again uses triple metre and a rising line for the image of lifting; its final two notes are then heard in bar 59 (Bt 103–4; St 85–6) for the word 'pauperem' (literally 'the poor man'). The conceit is clear. The psalm tone which had represented God in verses 4 and 5 here represents the poor man. If further evidence of the conceit were needed, it is provided in verse 7 – 'That he may set him with princes ...' – where the poor man, again represented by the psalm tone in the Quintus part (bars 62–7 (Bt 110–20; St 92–102)), is set prominently in the midst of a richly dissonant eight-part texture. The imagery of verse 8 is less abstruse: the psalm tone is maintained in the middle of the texture, in the Tenor, and the joy of the barren woman expressed by the use of triple metre. Triple metre is also a prominent feature of the 'Gloria Patri' in which Monteverdi contrasts four-part textures with a solo voice – the Quintus – who sings the psalm tone, also in triple metre. It is tempting to suggest that Monteverdi intended his conceit to be carried through to this point, as the poor man, set among princes in verse 7, now praises God.

'Lætatus sum'

'A sei voci.' The setting is in Mode 2 which, as usual for polyphony in this mode, is transposed up a fourth, as implied by the one-flat signature.[3] Monteverdi strengthens the sense of a G tonality by sharpening the penultimate F of the psalm tone. The tone is also transposed up a fourth. Only the principal cadence centres of G and D, and the 'quasi-principal' B flat, are used.

The setting of 'Lætatus sum' is a technical *tour de force*. At first hearing it appears not to conform with the principle that governs the other psalms of the 1610 collection since the psalm tone is clearly missing from the settings of verses 2, 3, 5, 9 and 10. Moreover, because of the variety of material and textures that Monteverdi invents, it is not easy at first to perceive that the structure is coherent.

For this psalm Monteverdi uses the technique of strophic variation, a technique employed by a number of the early writers of continuo song, among them Caccini in his *Le nuove musiche*; and it was one that Monteverdi himself used several times in *Orfeo* – for the Prologue, for example, for the choruses at the ends of Acts I and II, and for the great aria 'Possente spirto' in Act III. In a typical set of strophic variations each verse of the text is set to different music over a repeated bass-line, or at least over a repeated harmonic framework. In 'Lætatus sum', however, Monteverdi employs not one, but three interlocking sets of strophic variations over three apparently distinct basses, as shown in Table 5.2.

Bass A is the most frequently heard in the setting, and its jaunty crotchet movement also makes it the most memorable of the three basses. Despite their apparently distinct characteristics, however, all three are designed to harmonise the psalm tone, as Example 10 shows (Monteverdi retains the intonation of the psalm tone for statements of basses A and B (verses 1, 6, 7), but omits it for all statements of bass C (verses 4, 8, 11)). As Table 5.2 shows, however, Monteverdi plays games with the listener's expectations by sometimes omitting the psalm tone itself, allowing it to be represented by the bass alone – Enigma variations, as it were, in which the theme is present but unheard.

The pattern for the presence or absence of the psalm tone seems random if traced on a verse-by-verse basis, but is, in fact, related to each of the three sets of variations. The tone is present for each statement of bass C (indeed, its second phrase is heard twice, first in the Altus part, transposed to begin on F (see, for example, bars 43–6 (Bt 77–84)), then in the Cantus (bars 47–50 (Bt 85–92)) or Sextus (bars 89–92 and 117–19 (Bt 168–73 and 223–7; St 88–91 and 116–18)), beginning on B flat). The pattern for bass B is absent (verse 2) – present (verse 6) – absent (verse 10). And the pattern for bass A is present (verse 1) – absent (verses 3 and 5) – present (verse 7) – absent (verse 9). The unfinished pattern for bass A is also reflected in the pattern of scorings that Monteverdi chose for it, which increase steadily from one voice (verse 1) to four (verse 7) before jumping to six

Table 5.2

Bars	Verse	Bass	No. of voices	Part(s) bearing cantus firmus
1–9 (Bt 1–17)	1	A	1	T
9–20 (Bt 17–39)	2	B	6	—
20–8 (Bt 39–55)	3	A	2	—
29–50 (Bt 56–92)	4	C	6	C (section 1 of chant)
				A (section 2)
				C (section 2)
50–8 (Bt 92–108)	5	A	3	—
58–69 (Bt 108–29)	6	B	5	C
69–77 (Bt 130–46)	7	A	4	S
78–92 (Bt 147–73; St 78–91)	8	C	6	S (section 1 of chant)
				A (section 2)
				S (section 2)
92–100 (Bt 173–89; St 91–9)	9	A	6	—
100–111 (Bt 190–212; St 99–110)	10	B	6	—
112–21 (Bt 213–31; St 111–20)	11	C	6	C (section 1 of chant)
				A (section 2)
				S (section 2)

Ex. 10
Bass A (bars 3–5 (Bt 5–10))

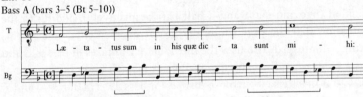

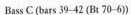

Bass B (bars 63–6 (Bt 118–23))

Bass C (bars 39–42 (Bt 70–6))

voices in verse 9. There is, on the face of it, no reason why he should not have chosen to follow through the pattern established for bass A, using five voices for verse 9 and then six for verse 11; indeed, using this bass for the last verse as well as the first would have provided an apt musical metaphor for the words 'As it was in the beginning'. Several considerations may have influenced Monteverdi's decision. If he had followed the pattern established for bass A, then the psalm tone would have been omitted for verse 11; using bass A instead of bass C would have meant that bass C would have been heard only twice in the composition as compared with three statements of bass B and five of bass A. Or it may be that the repeated I–V harmonies at the end of bass C appealed to him for the opportunity they presented of matching the text 'for ever and ever' by the use of repeated harmonies (see bars 115 and 117–18 (Bt 218–19 and 222–4; St 114 and 116–17)).

Because the transposed first phrase of the psalm tone focuses on, and cadences on B flat, rather than on G, Monteverdi constructs the three basses so that each begins with a passage that establishes the mode by cadencing on G or D before modulating to B flat. In the case of bass A this introductory passage is quite short (bars 1–2 (Bt 1–4)), but those for basses B and C (first two statements only) are more extended (five and eight-and-a-half bars respectively), adding to the impression that the psalm tone plays only an incidental role in this setting. Monteverdi also uses the introductory phrases of basses B and C as a contrast to the subsequent phrases of each bass. In the case of bass C this gives rise to virtuoso display, at bars 29–37 (Bt 62–7) and at bars 78–84 (Bt 147–57; St 78–83), where the bass underpins one of the most striking moments in the setting: an extended passage of Lombard rhythms on the word 'Propter' which has no counterpart elsewhere in the 1610 Vespers.[4] (The introductory phrase of bass C is omitted at the third statement of the bass (bars 112–19 (Bt 213–27; St 111–18)) and its second phrase reduced to a harmonic skeleton.)

The initial phrase of bass B is also very striking, for each time it is heard Monteverdi cancels out the staff signature of B flat, reinstating it only for the second and third phrases. His reason for doing this seems to have been inspired by the textual imagery of verses 1 and 2. The bass used for verse 1 – bass A, a lively 'walking bass' in crotchets, itself something of a novelty in 1610 – neatly encapsulates the ideas of

Ex. 11

movement and pleasure of 'I was glad when they said unto me: "Let us go into the house of the Lord"', while the use of a solo voice matches the use of the first-person singular. In contrast, the slow-moving rhythm of the beginning of bass B then provides a reasonably close musical match for the stillness of 'Our feet have been wont to stand [within thy gates, O Jerusalem]' and the use of six voices reflects the use of the plural; moreover, the use of a major, rather than a minor third above G – the major interval was already regarded as more cheerful than the minor[5] – suggests the pleasure afforded by the prospect of Jerusalem.

The phrases of bass B that follow, however, provide an opportunity for subtextual interpretation, for they are, in fact, the second and third phrases of the Romanesca bass, one of a family of ground-bass patterns used chiefly in a secular context for the setting of stanzas of Italian epic verse. If we compare the relevant phrases of bass B (bars 14–17 and 17–20 (Bt 27–33 and 33–9)) with those of Example 11, a Romanesca published in 1609 by one of the most notable of early composers of continuo song – Sigismondo d'India[6] – then the identity of Monteverdi's bass becomes unmistakable. It may be, too, that he omitted the psalm tone for this verse in order to draw attention to his use of the Romanesca, the shape of which is also imitated in the upper parts.

Why did Monteverdi use the Romanesca here? Was it simply to show off his inventiveness, by demonstrating that it could be used to harmonise Psalm Tone 2, a fact, however, which is only made explicit when we reach bars 63–9 (Bt 118–29)? Or did he, by linking Jerusalem with a bass associated with Rome, and one that would certainly have been readily recognised in the early seventeenth century, intend a subtle compliment to Rome and the papacy? The latter seems likely. The entire psalm text is, in fact, concerned with Jerusalem as the centre of the Nation of Israel, and by associating the Romanesca with the first mention of Jerusalem in verse 2 Monteverdi invites an interpretation of the text in terms of Rome as the centre of Christianity. And because basses A and C are also devised as basses for

Psalm Tone 2 and have some characteristics in common with bass B (see Ex. 10), they, too, reinforce this reinterpretation.

If this reading of the subtext is correct, then it has other implications for the Vespers as a whole. Did Monteverdi just happen upon the idea that the Romanesca could be used as a bass for Psalm Tone 2 and develop the interpretation Rome = Jerusalem from that happy discovery, or did he, as seems more likely, choose Psalm Tone 2 precisely because it lent itself to harmonisation by the Romanesca? If the latter, then this would be further evidence that the choice of Tone 2 for this psalm was dictated by compositional rather than liturgical considerations.

'Nisi Dominus'

'A dieci voci.' The setting is in Mode 6. In this case the staff signature of B flat does not (in eight-mode theory, at least) indicate transposition. Rather, it recognises that in a polyphonic composition the unwanted tritone F–B natural would otherwise figure prominently.[7] Psalm Tone 6 is presented untransposed in verses 1 to 4, transposed up a fourth in verses 5 and 6 and down a fifth from that for the 'Gloria Patri' before returning to the original pitch for 'Sicut erat in principio'. The intonation is retained in every verse (twice in verse 5) and the ending of the tone is slightly modified for tonal reasons. In general Monteverdi uses only the principal cadence centres of the mode – F and A – when the psalm tone is untransposed, with transitory cadences on D at bars 22 and 29 (Bt 44 and 58), but since he transposes the psalm tone twice he manages to reach the distant cadence of E flat at bar 89 (Bt 175; St 8) before dropping back to F.

'Nisi Dominus' is the only one of the 1610 psalms that does not begin with a solo intonation. Instead, we are presented with a massive ten-part texture, divided into two SATTB choirs, in which the psalm tone is sung by a tenor in each choir. The psalm tone is embedded in a busy texture characterised by canon at a crotchet's distance between Cantus, Tenor 2, Sextus and (after two initial notes) Quintus 1. A second canon begins between the two Altus parts, and a third, lasting two bars only, between the two bass parts. Needless to say, in such a dense texture, Monteverdi is unable to sustain the canons exactly for any length of time, but he manages to give the impression that the first, at least, lasts for most of the first half-verse; he then uses an inverted subject at the beginning of the second half-verse.

It is tempting to see in this imposing musical edifice and industrious, if not entirely satisfactory, building of canons a metaphor for the first verse of the psalm – 'Except the Lord build the house, they labour in vain that build it'. Equally, though, Monteverdi may simply have wanted to provide a full texture for the beginning (and the end, since he reuses the music for the end of the doxology) of a setting which proceeds for the most part in a dialogue between the two five-part choirs. The dialogue is rather unusual in terms of antiphonal psalmody. Rather than allotting each choir a verse in alternation, Monteverdi sets each verse for Choir 1 and then has Choir 2 repeat it, with a two-chord overlap at the end of each verse. The probable reason for doing this was to create a more substantial structure than would otherwise have been possible with a psalm whose main text is only six verses long, especially since Monteverdi sets verses 2–6 in energetic chant-like rhythms. Although there is little by way of madrigalian word-painting, there are some subtleties in the text setting. Verses 2–4 are treated as a unit, with a rhythmic progression from crotchets and minims (verse 2) through dotted rhythms (verse 3) to quaver passages (verse 4). The longer note values at the beginnings of each phrase highlight important words in the text – 'nisi' (except), 'frustra' (in vain), 'vanum' ([it is] vain) – and the phrase 'frustra vigilat' (waketh in vain) is emphasised by repetition in bars 24–5 (Bt 47–9).

At the beginning of verse 5 Monteverdi moves from a reciting note of A to one of D, though he drops back to A at bar 67 in preparation for the overlap between choirs. Verses 5 and 6, which express warlike imagery, are both set in triple metre, leading to overlapping fanfare-like exchanges over a dominant–tonic bass for 'he shall not be confounded when he speaketh with his enemies in the gate'; this is a passage which foreshadows by more than a decade the use of similar motifs in Monteverdi's *stile concitato*. His decision to begin the doxology with the psalm tone transposed down a fifth from the level reached at the end of the psalm was a stroke of genius. The doxology could so easily have seemed an anticlimax after the rhythmic vitality of the earlier verses. Instead, the opulent E flat harmony on which it begins and the sudden emergence of the initial music and tonality of the psalm for 'As it was in the beginning' are both a surprise and a delight.

The double-choir dialogue of 'Nisi Dominus', implying the use of choirs spatially separated, has often been taken to relate the setting to the practice of St Mark's, Venice. In fact, though, the use of double-choir settings was as much a Mantuan or Roman as a Venetian practice[8] and, as we now know, while double-choir motets were performed at St Mark's using spatially separated choirs, double-choir psalms were performed there with both ensembles in the same location – one of the large pulpits located in front of the choir screen.[9]

'Lauda Ierusalem'

'A Sette voci.' The setting is in Mode 3. Psalm Tone 3 appears untransposed in verses 1–3, 7–9, and the doxology (bars 59–62 of verse 10, and verse 11) and transposed a fourth higher, to F, in verses 4–6, and in bars 54–9 and 63–5 of verse 10. The intonation of the psalm tone is used for verse 1 only. Monteverdi uses only two of the principal cadence centres of the mode – A and C (the median cadence of the psalm tone; D and F when the psalm tone is transposed). Cadences on E, the final of the mode, are not used.

As in 'Nisi Dominus' Monteverdi employs the technique of musical dialogue for the main body of this setting, with exchanges between two trios of soprano, alto and bass around the psalm tone, which is presented verse by verse in the tenor. After the opening verse he divides the text into three sections – verses 2–3, 4–6 and 7–9 – reserving his most complex and exciting textures for the last section. In the exchanges between the ensembles the soprano acts as the leading voice, with the other two serving as more or less imitative fillers. In the first section the impression is of a single melodic line passed between Cantus and Sextus, the phrases of which are linked by a motif spanning a falling fourth (Ex. 12), presented in one rhythmic guise in bars 10, 12 and 16 (Bt 20, 23–4 and 32), and in another in the extended final phrase, bars 19–21 (Bt 37–41). The second section, beginning at bar 21 (Bt 42), is marked by a sudden shift from the chord of A to that of F, and the transposition of the psalm tone to a reciting note of F. In this section the phrase-lengths of the exchanges are halved, on average,

Ex. 12

Ex. 13

and a real sense of dialogue created in verses 5 and 6 (bars 24ff. (Bt 48ff.)) as Monteverdi divides statement and simile between the two groups (Ex. 13). The beginning of the third section is marked by another harmonic change of gear from D to F (bars 33–4 (Bt 66–7)) and the psalm tone is returned to its original pitch. In this section the two trios echo each other, with a canon between Cantus and Sextus at only a semibreve's distance, producing a full texture relieved by a very striking elongation of the harmonic rhythm at bars 37–9 (Bt 74–8) at the words 'et fluent aquæ' (and the waters flow) and culminating in a series of imitations at only a minim's distance from bar 45 (Bt 89), producing a quasi-canonic texture very like the beginning of 'Nisi Dominus'.

Once again, verse 1 and the doxology are treated independently. The psalm opens with an ear-catching command and choral response prefacing the solo statement of each half of the psalm tone. After the busy texture of verse 9, the much broader opening of the doxology (bar 54 (Bt 107)) provides an impressive contrast, with the first half of the psalm tone in long notes high in the Cantus and its transposition to F allowing a rich B flat harmony in bar 55 (Bt 110 – F major, because of the transposition). The second half of the doxology re-establishes the psalm tone firmly on C, heard in Sextus, Bassus, then Quintus and Sextus; in this verse all the voices join in the chant rhythm, which then issues into a highly expressive, imitative Amen.

'Ave maris stella'

'Hymnus à 8.' The instrumentation of the ritornelli is not specified. Monteverdi's use of plainsong is seen at its most straightforward in the exquisite double-choir setting of the hymn 'Ave maris stella'; the main interest here lies in identifying whether the melody that he used is drawn from a Roman or a Santa Barbara source (see the discussion in Chapter 3, pp. 33–4).

Monteverdi treats the plainsong essentially as a melody to be har-monised. In verses 2 to 6 of the hymn, for example, it is transformed into triple metre, placed at the top of the texture and presented as a simple melody sung to the same harmonies for each verse. Only the scoring changes from verse to verse – Choir 1 à 4, Choir 2 à 4, Cantus (i.e. Choir 1 soprano) solo, Sextus (Choir 2 soprano) solo, Tenor (Choir 1) solo – and the verses are separated by a triple-metre ritornello for five unnamed instruments and continuo. The ritornello, though apparently distinct from the hymn verses, shares their triple metre and division into four phrases. There are other links, too. The rising line at the beginning of the second phrase, and the descending line leading to the cadence of phrase 3 characterise both hymn and ritornello; and in both cases the third phrase leads to a very striking cadence on C, a tonal centre which is not 'proper' to Mode 1.

In the eight-part setting used for verses 1 and 8 the plainsong is somewhat disguised, though it is still treated as harmonised melody. It is presented in duple metre in the soprano part of Choir 1 (Cantus) over a harmonic bass that is essentially the same as that used for verses 2 to 6. Against the hymn melody, however, Monteverdi sets a counter-melody in the soprano of Choir 2 (Sextus) which lies generally higher than the plainsong and thus draws attention from it. The accompany-ing texture, too, is rather more than a simple filling in of the harmony. In the first phrase, for example, the beginning of the counter-melody in the Sextus part is shadowed in shorter note values in the tenor of Choir 1 and the alto of Choir 2, while the rising scale of the plainsong (bars 2–3 (Bt 3–5)) is shadowed by the bass of Choir 2. And in each of the first three phrases the Quintus part (Choir 2 tenor) imitates or prefigures details from other lines – the rising fifth of the plainsong (bar 1), the initial intervals of the counter-melody (bars 2–3 (Bt 4–6)), the shape of pitches 4–7 of the second phrase of the plainsong (bars 6–

7 (Bt 11–14)) and, with added pitches, the outline of the plainsong
phrase that it accompanies in bars 10–11 (Bt 20–3; St 10–12).

The Magnificat settings

'Sex vocibus' (six-part setting); 'Septem vocibus, & sex Instrumentis'
(seven-part setting). The instruments specified for the seven-part setting are: three cornetts, two violins, and one *viuola da brazzo*, but,
additionally, two *fifare*, two trombones and two flutes are required for
'Quia respexit', and a single trombone for 'Sicut locutus est'. Both
settings are in Mode 1 transposed to G. The psalm tone is used both
in its transposed form, beginning on B flat, and at its original pitch of
F. Generally speaking the pitch level is the same for corresponding
verses in the two settings; there are, however, differences in verses 4, 5
and 8. In general Monteverdi restricts himself to the principal cadence
centres of G, D and B flat, and the few excursions to F tend to occur in
those verses in which the *cantus firmus* is presented untransposed.
What is more remarkable about both settings, the seven-part one in
particular, is the inclusion of performance indications, suggesting that
the Magnificats at least had been performed prior to publication. In
both, the organ registration is marked at the beginning of each section,
sometimes more frequently.[10] Several sections include instructions for
changes of dynamics: in the seven-part 'Quia respexit', for example, a
rubric instructs that the obbligato instruments should play 'as loudly
as possible'; in its six-part equivalent, as the organ registration is
marked up to 'Principale, ottava & quintadecima' for 'omnes gene-
rationes', the singer is instructed to sing 'forte'. And in several sections involving short note values – verses 2, 4 and 9 of the seven-part
version, and verse 5 of the six-part version – a rubric instructs that
these sections should be taken more slowly. Curiously, there are no
such rubrics for the most virtuosic sections – verses 7 and 11 of the
seven-part version, verse 7 of the six-part version. The seven-part
version, however, contains a notational quirk which may itself indicate
that some sections should be taken slower than others. In all the vocal
and instrumental parts, the signature for *integer valor* is ₵. In the
Bassus generalis book, however, and simultaneously with the ₵ signature in the upper parts, verses 3, 5, 6, 8 and 12 are notated with the
signature ₵. A very plausible explanation for this inconsistency has

been offered by Roger Bowers, who observed that the signature ¢, while nominally meaning movement at twice the speed of C, was actually interchangeable with it, and indicated a 'tactus celerior', 'a quickish beat' as distinct from the 'tactus tardior' ('a slowish beat') for C. Thus, verses 2, 4, 7 and 9–11, which include the most virtuosic sections as well as those with a verbal instruction to take a slower tempo, are all to be taken at a moderate speed, while verses 1, 3, 5–6, 8 and 12 may be taken faster. The inconsistent signatures appear in the *Bassus generalis* book only since this was the book used by the organist (and choirmaster, if these were two separate people).[11]

The Magnificat forms the climax (though not the end) of Vespers, during which the altar is ceremonially censed. Both the six- and the seven-part versions in the 1610 print reflect the importance of this moment, by being expansive settings in which each verse of the canticle is allotted its own texture; the seven-part setting with six instruments, the version heard most often in concert and on record, lasts more than twice as long in performance as the longest of the psalms. As only a cursory glance will show, the two settings are related. Hans Redlich suggested that the six-part version was scaled down from the seven-part. More recently, however, Jeffrey Kurtzman has presented a more detailed analysis and argued persuasively that the six-part version is the earlier of the two, the seven-part setting being developed from it.[12] On the whole, Monteverdi tends to expand the material taken from the six-part version, though the adaptation of verse 1 involves a tightening of the structure, with the discrete phrases of bars 1–8 of the six-part version being turned into overlapping phrases and the vocal duet reduced to a shorter solo. Kurtzman's analysis shows a relationship between no fewer than ten sections of the two settings; the exceptions are verses 9 and 11. In some cases the relationships are immediately obvious, as in the case of verses 1–3, 8 and 12. Sometimes the relationships are more difficult to establish – the main correspondences between the settings of verse 6 in the two versions are found in the bass lines – or are even displaced: verse 4 of the six-part version seems to correspond to verse 5 of the seven-part and vice versa.

One further aspect of the two settings, not noted by Kurtzman, supports his contention that the seven-part version is the later of the two. This is that Monteverdi omits the passing note G (C in the transposed form used by Monteverdi) from the termination of

Ex. 14

the psalm tone in the seven-part setting (compare, for example, bars 10–11 of the six-part setting (not in Bt & St) with bar 10 (Bt 19–20; St 7) of the seven-part). As far as I can tell this is a compositional decision and not a case of Monteverdi's using a different plainsong source. Its effect is to reshape the end of the plainsong to draw attention to the repeat and extension of the three-note phrase A–G–F (D–C–B flat in transposition) (Ex. 14); it also produces a focal point within the line which is lacking in the more leisurely full presentation of the plainsong. It further introduces into the Magnificat *cantus firmus* the prominent leap of a third which also characterises the openings of 'Laudate pueri', 'Lætatus sum' and 'Lauda Ierusalem', and the second phrase of the version of the 'Ave maris stella' melody that Monteverdi used.

Monteverdi's verse-by-verse setting produces rather diffuse structures which are perfectly satisfactory as accompaniments to a liturgical action, but rather harder to appreciate in terms of musical architecture. In the seven-part Magnificat, however, it seems that Monteverdi attempted to introduce an overall symmetry lacking in the six-part version (yet another argument for the seven-part version being the product of second thoughts). The identification of symmetrical structures, it must be said, depends to some extent on the specific elements being observed, and Kurtzman and Bowers arrive at different schemes, Bowers's taking in only the first ten verses of the setting, while Kurtzman's embraces all twelve.[13] Certainly there are very strong similarities between the openings of verses 1 and 12 in terms of scoring, tonality and the use of the psalm tone in imitation between Cantus and Sextus. The parallels that Kurtzman defines between verses 2 and 11 and 3 and 10 are also convincing, so that the sense of solid pillars at the two ends of the setting remains, even though the symmetries between the inner verses are, perhaps, more loosely drawn (see Table 5.3).

The styles and textures that Monteverdi chose for individual sections of the seven-voice Magnificat can often be explained only in terms of musical invention. Some at least, however, probably took their initial impulse from the text. The grand setting of the word

Table 5.3

Verse	Scoring	Kurtzman's definitions
1	7vv + 6 insts	Chorus followed by solo soprano
2	3vv	Virtuoso duet for tenors
3	1v + 6 insts (more instruments are called called for during the course of this section than are mentioned in the rubric)	Ritornello structure and paired obbligato instruments
4	3vv + 2 insts	Virtuoso duet for basses with two obbligato violins
5	6vv	Two vocal trios in dialogue
6	1v + 3 insts	Duet for violins
7	1v + 4 insts	Echo duets for cornetti and violins
8	2vv + 4 insts	Ritornello structure with Magnificat tone in parallel thirds in two voices
9	3vv	Virtuoso duet for sopranos
10	1v + 6 insts	Dialogue between paired obbligato instruments
11	3vv	Virtuoso duet for tenors
12	7vv + 6 insts	Chorus

'Magnificat' after the initial intonation is a case in point: the Latin word order, with the verb placed first, then allows Monteverdi to drop down to a more intimate solo presentation of the Virgin's words. Similarly, the energetic rhythms of verse 2 can be taken as representing 'Exsultavit' (rejoiced), the longer note values of 'Et misericordia' (verse 5) the idea of mercy (cf. a similar contrast in verse 9 at the word 'misericordiæ'), and the 'empty' two-part vocal texture of 'Esurientes' (verse 8) the hungry who are to be filled with good things. The most striking sections in this respect are, however, verses 7 and 11, both of which use echo effects and virtuoso writing for, respectively, instruments and voices. There are very clear parallels between the virtuoso instrumental writing of verse 7 and the instrumental interjections in the aria 'Possente spirto' of Monteverdi's *Orfeo* and between the vocal line of 'Possente spirto' and the almost oriental cantillation over a slow-moving bass that characterises the vocal lines of verse 11. We have already encountered musical metaphors involving virtuoso singing in 'Duo Seraphim' and 'Laudate pueri'; its use for praise of the Trinity in verse 11 is not surprising; perhaps the metaphor intended in verse 7 is that the high art of the instrumentalists is what the mighty lose and the humble gain.

Certain characteristics of these extraordinarily inventive settings allow one to speculate further on the dates of their composition. As we noted earlier, Monteverdi's reuse of material from *Orfeo* in the opening response certainly dates its composition to 1607 or later, and the similarity between sections of the seven-part Magnificat and passages of 'Possente spirto' suggest a similar dating. But Monteverdi's decision to set the first psalm of the collection – 'Dixit Dominus' – as an elaboration of the standard plainsong–*falsobordone* alternation of a simple Vespers service, and his apparent compliment to Rome in 'Lætatus sum', suggest that both settings may have been written after he had conceived the idea of publishing a portfolio of sacred music, probably after 1608. In fact, the only ensemble music in the collection that seems much earlier in style is the seamless counterpoint of 'Lauda Ierusalem'. Jeffrey Kurtzman has also shown that the musical texts of 'Lauda Ierusalem' and 'Nisi Dominus' contain fewer errors than the other contents of the 1610 print; this argues that they had been composed earlier and the manuscript copies corrected after experience in rehearsal and performance.[14] Adding these considerations to what we can glean from our knowledge of Monteverdi's career at Mantua, I would suggest that the 1610 Vespers music was not written as a unit; that, nevertheless, most, if not all the settings date from after Monteverdi's appointment as court choirmaster in 1601; and that perhaps half or more of the ensemble pieces were written after the crisis of 1608.[15]

6

Issues of performance

Strictly speaking, the modern revival of interest in Monteverdi's 1610 Vespers dates from 1834, when Carl von Winterfeld, one of the founding fathers of historical musicology, published transcriptions of the opening of 'Dixit Dominus' and the 'Deposuit' section of the seven-part Magnificat to illustrate his extended discussion of the 1610 publication.[1] In the early years of this century the 'Sonata sopra Sancta Maria' was published in modern editions by Luigi Torchi (Milan, 1907)[2] and, in a 'versione ritmica e strumentale', by Bernardino Molinari (Milan, 1919). But it was not until 1932, when it appeared in Gian Francesco Malipiero's collected edition of Monteverdi's works, that all the 1610 Vespers music was made available, and not until February 1935 that it was revived in performance in Zürich, and then at Winterthur and Lausanne, by the Häusermann Privatchor under Hermann Dubs.[3] The edition used for these performances was prepared from Malipiero's by Hans Redlich, and it formed the basis of a number of other first performances of the Vespers over the following decade: in New York under Hugh Ross (1937); on Radio Beromünster (Switzerland) under Hermann Scherchen (early and mid-1940s); in Brussels under Paul Collaer (1946); and at Central Hall, Westminster, London, under Walter Goehr (14 May 1946).[4] The last of these was organised by the composer Michael Tippett, who also wrote his *Preludio al Vespro di Monteverdi* for the performance in order to help the choir find their first notes.[5]

Malipiero's approach to editing the 1610 Vespers had been simply to score up what he found in the original printed part-books, and for that reason, though his edition contains a number of errors, it has remained a serviceable study score through the various cycles of interpretation and elaboration that have been applied to the Vespers by scholars and performers over the past sixty years. Redlich's view, however, was that Malipiero's edition, despite its importance, 'can never be used as the basis of practical performances. The realization of the Basso Continuo ... is only roughly drafted; the apportioning of the instruments is entirely lacking'; he also took the view that the Vespers was merely an appendage to the Mass and constituted a 'fortuitous grouping together as a unit' which 'implies no further mutual obligation with regard to performance'.[6] In his own performing edition, therefore, he omitted the psalms 'Nisi Dominus' and 'Lauda Ierusalem', rearranged the remainder into what he considered a satisfactory order of performance (1, 2, 6, 4, 3, 7, 5, 9, 12, 11, 13, to use the numbering of the Discography, below), orchestrated the psalms and Magnificat generally for modern instruments (though he also composed a viola da gamba obbligato for 'Pulchra es'), worked out an elaborate scheme of solos and tuttis, doubled the vocal lines where the instrumental parts were 'missing', provided an often very intricate continuo realisation, and larded the score with tempo and dynamic marks. The danger that an edition of this kind might mislead even a seasoned and wary listener is reflected in the report of the music critic of *The Times*, who said of the 1946 London performance:

> The text used last night was Malipiero's ... but the assignment of instrumental ritornelli now to strings, now to brass, the decision when to use organ and when harpsichord and all such matters of distribution were the work of Dr. Hans Redlich, and though without a score it is impossible to say what licence he has allowed himself in such a feature as the ravishing addition to orchestral tones of half a dozen recorder flutes, the ear certainly received few jolts of doubt and the alto 'Audi coelum with its gamba obbligato [originally the vocal echoes in the solo section] recalled the bigger declamatory arias [of Monteverdi's *Orfeo*].[7]

A recording of Redlich's edition under Hans Grischkat was issued in 1953 and was immediately attacked in a review by Leo Schrade, who had published a full-scale study of Monteverdi some three years earlier, and whose own edition was used for the 1953 recording under Anthony Lewis, the first 'complete' recording of the Vespers.[8] Schrade began:

> Recently there have been a good many performances of Monteverdi's works, especially numerous in the case of the Vespers, in concerts and over the radio, and all of them so remarkably remote in spirit and letter from Monteverdi's original that the time seems to have come for frank

criticism. For arbitrary, inartistic performances will, in time, seriously affect understanding for Monteverdi's work. ... The recording of Monteverdi's Vespers, here reviewed, shows all the deplorable features we have mentioned: a version over-romantic, with little musical taste and understanding of style, but with serious changes in the original text. The deviations from the original are indeed so serious that they can no longer be regarded as legitimate 'interpretations' but must be qualified as arrangements, violating both scholarship and musicianship.[9]

He continued by making a detailed critique of the methods used by Redlich and also stated his own view of the Vespers as

a perfect unity, both liturgical and artistic ... Monteverdi's intention is perfectly clear. With each composition he presented a different medium and, at the same time, a different aspect of the modern style; never is there any repetition of the medium in the Vespers as a whole; thus they are a grandiose synopsis of all that Monteverdi had achieved in 1610 in founding the new style.

Schrade's own, less intrusive, edition, which also corrected errors in Malipiero's transcription, unfortunately remained unpublished. Redlich, meanwhile, continued to defend his position, not least by attacking Schrade's 'fundamentalist' position, the 'excessively fast tempos' of the Lewis recording and the 'preposterous' use of a solo soprano for the 'Sonata sopra Sancta Maria' in Lewis's broadcast performances of 19 and 21 February 1954.[10] He also revised his own edition to include all the Vespers music. This was made available in manuscript in 1955 by Universal Edition of Vienna, and published in 1958 by Bärenreiter of Kassel. By this time, however, Redlich's was not the only available performing edition. As early as 1952 a condensed elaboration for chorus, [soloists] and orchestra, omitting numbers 4–9 and tacitly including Monteverdi's solo motet 'O quam pulchra es' from a Venetian anthology of 1625, had been issued by Giorgio Ghedini (Milan: Suvini Zerboni); it was recorded under Stokowski in 1955. And in Britain, Walter Goehr had gone on to make his own elaboration for performance, which was widely used by choral societies and thus influential in introducing many listeners to the music, and in shaping their attitudes towards it, though it was not recorded until 1970, and then without the Magnificat.

Up to the end of the 1950s those editors who had omitted items from the Vespers in their editions had done so as a matter of personal preference or from practical considerations. Little had been done to explore the relationship of Monteverdi's collection to the liturgy of Vespers, though in his 1950 book on Monteverdi, Leo Schrade had suggested the possibility that the sacred concertos might have been intended as antiphon-substitutes. In 1961, however, the question of liturgy was brought centre stage by Denis Stevens, who argued in a major article that the concertos formed no part of the official liturgy of Vespers.[11] He also suggested that the smaller, six-part version of the Magnificat was for use at First Vespers and the larger seven-part version at Second Vespers. He was one of the first commentators to question the assumption that the ensemble pieces in the Vespers were necessarily Venetian in style, and also one of the first to question the need for large forces in performing them. His ideas were also summarised in a smaller article[12] and in the preface to his new edition of the Vespers music (London, 1961) which, following the logic of his argument, omitted the concertos.[13] He directed performances of his edition at Westminster Abbey on 14 and 15 July 1961 and issued a recording in 1967. Stevens's view that the concertos should be omitted from editions and performances of the 1610 Vespers was challenged in 1967 by Stephen Bonta[14] (see above, pp. 17–18), and subsequent editions, including Stevens's revised (1994) version, have all included the concertos.

Performance with period instruments

Stevens continued the editorial tradition of dividing the musical fabric of the psalms and Magnificat between soloists and chorus and doubling vocal lines with instruments. His edition used (and still uses) modern instruments, substituting oboes for the cornetti, rather than the more usual trumpets. The use of modern instruments continued for some time to be the norm in Vespers performances. They were employed, for example, by John Eliot Gardiner for the performance at King's College Cambridge on 5 March 1964 which launched his career as a conductor, and they can be heard on the 1974 recording which represents his early view of the Vespers. The 1960s, however, saw a growing interest in exploring the performance practice of early music and, in particular, in reviving the techniques of playing on period instruments, whether originals or reconstructions. By the time of the quatercentenary of Monteverdi's birth in 1967 a recording had been issued which claimed to re-create the sound-world of the early seventeenth century, particularly in terms of the instruments used, though it also introduced singers like Nigel Rogers, who could actually sing Monteverdi's *trilli* in a convincing manner. This was the 1966/67 recording under Jürgens, featuring Nikolaus Harnoncourt's Concentus Musicus of Vienna. At the time this seemed revelatory, and its spacious quality, emphasising the ethereal, rather than the exciting, is still very attractive.

Although Jürgens's recording marked a turning point in performances of the 1610 Vespers, in some ways it still reflected long-accepted attitudes towards the work. Performances up to this time (and for many years afterwards) took as their starting point the idea that the Vespers was a work for choir and soloists, with choral forces at least of the size of a present-day cathedral choir, and sometimes much larger. Monteverdi's part-books, which do not specify contrasts between choir and soloists, were thus considered to provide only a skeleton, which needed to be interpreted by the editor or editor-performer. The same applied to the instrumental forces involved. Aside from the continuo accompaniment, the 1610 part-books specify instruments only for the opening response, 'Dixit Dominus', the 'Sonata sopra Sancta Maria', 'Ave maris stella' and the seven-part Magnificat. This instrumentation, too, was regarded only as a skeleton which needed to be filled out by instrumental doubling of vocal lines and, again, the extent to which this was done reflected the judgement of the editor or editor-performer. It also meant that the sound-world of performances varied widely and that the choice for performers seemed to be between using a ready-made performing edition such as those by Goehr or Stevens (or, from 1977, Jürgens's own edition),[15] or facing long hours of pre-rehearsal preparation.

The general currency of this view of the Vespers was also reflected in a new scholarly edition of the work by Gottfried Wolters (Wolfenbüttel, 1966). Although Wolters presented the main text of the Vespers music in a refreshingly clean form, he still felt it necessary to include an appendix showing how individual movements could be 'orchestrated'. For some performers, this view of the 1610 Vespers has continued to be valid; it informs, for example, the 1989 recordings under Harry Christophers, Frieder Bernius and Jordi Savall, and John Eliot Gardiner's second recording, a tightly controlled, and in many respects very exciting, performance, using period instruments and recorded in St Mark's, Venice.

Performance with solo voices

It is not surprising that the earliest attempts to recapture the sound quality of the early seventeenth century should have focused on instrumental sound, since instruments of the period had survived and could be copied. Moreover, the array of unfamiliar instruments was itself appealing to audiences, a fact reflected in the booklet accompanying Jürgens's recording. The process of trying to re-create late Renaissance vocal techniques from verbal descriptions alone inevitably proceeded more slowly and tentatively. Nevertheless, the growth of interest in early music in recent decades has enabled a number of singers to specialise in this area, with the result that there has been a shift towards less opulent, voice-centred, performances of the 1610 Vespers. Moreover, the thirty years which separate Jürgens's recording from the present day have also witnessed fundamental rethinking of other aspects of performance practice, some of which are still live, and highly contentious issues.

As early as 1967 Denis Arnold had begun publicly to question the need to divide the ensemble settings between chorus and soloists:

> I, for one, have never been convinced that it is necessary to divide the sections of various psalms between solo and tutti, still less that one should sing the canti fermi with a choir while other parts can be allotted to solo voices. Nor am I happy with the idea of singing the cantus in the *Sonata sopra Sancta Maria* chorally, and have suggested my own solution to the problem [in 'Monteverdi's Church Music: some Venetian Traits']. It seems to me quite possible to perform all the concertante music with an expert group of soloists and single instruments, leaving the choir to sing the opening versicle and the *cori spezzati* psalms.[16]

The question of whether parts or, indeed, the whole of the 1610 Vespers should be performed by solo voices is a difficult one, and is complicated by the fact that we do not know whether all the music was written for the same circumstances. Monteverdi's own statements are not unequivocal. His rubric 'à 8 voci sole nel Organo' for 'Laudate pueri' may simply indicate that this psalm, in contrast to 'Dixit Dominus', is for voices and organ alone, without obbligato instruments; the same applies to the rubric 'à 6 voci sole' for the 'Et misericordia' section of the seven-part Magnificat. On the other hand, the rubrics 'ad una voce sola & sei instrumenti' for both the 'Quia respexit' and 'Sicut locutus est' sections of the seven-part Magnificat, and 'ad una voce sola' for the 'Quia respexit' of the six-part Magnificat (in which, of course, no obbligato instruments are used), seem to point to soloist as against more than one voice per part. These rubrics apart, however, there are no other indications of solo-choir divisions in the Vespers music.

Another way of approaching the question would be to ask about the performing practice of particular chapels. The problem here, of course, is that we do not know for certain in which chapels Monteverdi's music was sung; and the same problem applies to trying to decide whether the double-choir items would have been sung with the choirs spaced apart. If some or all the music was performed in Santa Barbara, Mantua, then we know that the choir there numbered between six and eight professional singers – enough to sing double-choir music using solo voices. If the music were sung at Santa Barbara or some other Mantuan church by the duke's court virtuosi, then it is likely that the singers would have performed sacred music as they sang madrigals – one to a part, though with castrati singing the soprano lines and the alto part probably taken by a high tenor. Indeed, the ornamental patterns which Monteverdi uses and which seem to call for virtuosi are best performed by solo voices and instruments. The plainsong of the liturgy would, presumably, have been allocated to another body of singers.

If we imagine the music sung at one of the major churches in Rome (though not in the Sistine Chapel, where unaccompanied singing was cultivated) then the evidence (though not uncontested) again seems to point to the use of one singer per part, with singers taking it in turns in the larger choirs and extra singers being drafted in to the smaller as necessary when polychoral music was performed. A document of 1595 also mentions the use of instruments:

> On a feast, when a *maestro* brings together musicians for two Vespers and a Mass, he will invite members of the papal chapel, and instruments such as cornett, trombones, violins and lutes.[17]

The Cappella Giulia – the choir of St Peter's – comprised about eighteen singers (as compared with twenty-four active singers in the Cappella Sistina); if Monteverdi's music had been performed here (or at San Giovanni in Laterano, the pope's church as Bishop of Rome) then the soprano lines might have been taken by boys, unless we assume that Cappella Sistina castrati were drafted in for the occasion.

Finally, if we assume that Monteverdi might have used some of the Vespers music after his appointment to St Mark's, Venice, then he would have been able in 1616 to draw on a choir of twenty-four singers and an instrumental ensemble of eighteen players. We should not, however, assume that all these singers were available for any given service. Absenteeism was a problem at St Mark's, partly because some choir members were also priests at other churches, partly because they were sometimes called away to singing duties elsewhere (for the doge, or at other Venetian institutions).[18]

The evidence, though not conclusive, certainly encourages the view that all Monteverdi's 1610 Vespers music can, and probably should, be performed with one singer and one instrumentalist per part. The recordings that have been prepared on this basis – Pickett (1991), The Scholars (1995), Junghänel (1995/6) – demonstrate that whatever may be lost in terms of magnificence, there are great gains in terms of subtlety of expression, balance and definition and, in the case of the first two recordings, the excitement of the faster tempi possible with a small group of singers schooled in the singing styles and techniques of the period.

Instrumental accompaniment

As far as professional performances are concerned, the question of whether or not to use modern instruments is no longer an issue: period instruments are now assumed as standard, though the question of which instruments to use and how to dispose them still raises questions.[19] Less obviously, a revolution has also taken place in the continuo department. Whereas in early revivals of the Vespers the harpsichord was used for continuo accompaniment alongside the organ, its place has now been taken by the chitarrone or other similar large lute. The chitarrone, theorbo and arch-lute (the terms were sometimes used interchangeably) were favoured instruments for accompanying solo songs in the early seventeenth century (Caccini, for example, accompanied himself on the instrument when performing his songs); the use of these lutes in church is frequently documented, the use of the harpsichord less so;[20] and, above all, Monteverdi is known to have favoured organ and chitarrone/theorbo in combination for continuo accompaniments.[21] The other instrument that has largely disappeared from the continuo group is a bowed-string instrument doubling the bass line. Recent research suggests that such doubling was the exception rather than the rule in the early and mid-seventeenth century.[22]

If the music is to be sung by soloists, should their parts be doubled by instruments? The evidence for instrumental doubling springs chiefly from the Renaissance practice of allowing vocal music to be performed by voices and instruments together, and from recommendations for instrumental doubling made by a non-Italian writer, Michael Praetorius. But much of the 1610 music is not in the style of Renaissance polyphony, and it is unlikely that virtuoso vocalists would have welcomed having their lines doubled by instrumentalists, whether in the concertos or in the psalms. Moreover, on the one occasion in the Vespers when Monteverdi does require instruments to double vocal lines – in the 'Sicut erat' section of the Magnificat à 7 – he states this in a rubric – 'tutti li instrumenti & voci, & va cantato & sonato forte' (all the instruments and voices, to be sung and played *forte*) – and he provides the necessary instrumental parts in the printed part-books.

Transposition

Two further matters are very much live issues. The first concerns Monteverdi's use of high clefs in 'Lauda Ierusalem' and the two Magnificat settings. Whereas most of the Vespers settings use a combination of clefs for the vocal parts in which the sopranos were notated in C_1 clefs and the bass in an F_4 clef, 'Lauda Ierusalem' and the Magnificats were notated with the sopranos in a G_2 clef and the bass in F_3 and the intermediate voices also notated in higher clefs than usual. The vocal tessituras of these two movements are also, on average, higher than those of the other Vespers movements. It is highly likely that these high-clef movements would have been transposed down a fourth in performance. The need to transpose 'Lauda Ierusalem' and the Magnificats was first signalled by Jeffrey Kurtzman,[23] and the complex evidence fully and convincingly marshalled in an article by Andrew Parrott, to which Kurtzman added a further contribution.[24] Three recordings of the Vespers transpose these two movements down a fourth – Parrott's own (1984), Philippe Herreweghe's (1987) and Philip Pickett's (1991). Objections have been raised by performers and critics who, while feeling intuitively that downward transposition is correct for 'Lauda Ierusalem', consider that the Magnificat should be performed at written pitch (a) in order to produce a sense of climax, and (b) because the 'Et misericordia' section of the Magnificat à 7 seems too low. This has led to a number of recordings which attempt a halfway house (Savall, 1989, The Scholars, 1995, Junghänel, 1995/6). Intuition is not, however, evidence, and though an attempt to adduce such evidence was made in 1992 in an (as yet) unpublished paper by Stephen Bonta, Parrott has already produced a rebuttal in a further article on the subject in which he also looked briefly at the related, but largely unexplored subject of pitch standards in early seventeenth-century Italy.[25] Pitch standards at this period varied even between different Italian cities and we cannot as yet say what was the standard in Mantua. What we can say is that the idea that high = climactic is an anachronism: there was a predilection for low sonorities in Monteverdi's time.

Tempo and proportions

The second cause of dissension arises over the question of proportional relationships between passages in duple and triple metre in the Vespers. As in the case of transposition the evidence and arguments are too complex to be easily summarised without over-simplification. The tendency in most recent performances of the Vespers has been to take all passages in triple metre at a relatively fast speed, either by ignoring the idea that Monteverdi might have intended an exact proportional relationship between passages in duple and triple metre, or by assuming a single relationship in which, for example, three minims in triple metre are taken in the time of one in duple metre (see, for example, the change at bars 44–5 (Bt 48–9; St actually notates this relationship) of 'Domine ad adiuvandum', where such a relationship produces a very fast triple metre). This tendency in performances flows from two premises: first, that triple metre should always 'dance', and second, that the strict proportional relationships that governed the mensural system of notation had largely broken down by 1600. In a recent article, however, Roger Bowers argued persuasively that in the Vespers Monteverdi in fact still used the mensural system of proportions.[26] Under this system our example would produce the relationship 'three minims in triple are taken in the time of two minims in duple', producing a much broader triple metre. Bowers's arguments have been attacked by Kurtzman[27] and the effects of his conclusions have yet to be convincingly demonstrated in a recorded performance,[28] but the proportions that he suggests are shown in the critical commentary of the recent edition of the Vespers by Jerome Roche and taken into account in the critical commentary of Bartlett's edition, produced shortly after Bowers had first communicated his ideas at a conference in 1990.

Liturgical and concert performance

Most of the recordings mentioned so far, even those that include antiphons for the psalms and Magnificat, are essentially concert performances of the 1610 Vespers. As was argued earlier, this approach to performing the work is justifiable in that it reflects the nature of the 1610 publication as a portfolio of Monteverdi's work, published for the world to admire. It is doubly justified since, when Monteverdi published his collection, he chose to unify it by including only settings of psalms, hymn and Magnificat that were based on an unusually rigorous use of plainsong, and to lay them out, together with the sacred concertos, in the form of Vespers of the Madonna. Early seventeenth-century musicians who took the trouble to score up the music that the publication contained would have been able to admire these qualities, and our modern concert performances are the equivalent of their reading through the collection. However, Monteverdi would not have expected his music to be performed in this way since there was no forum in the early seventeenth century in which the complete collection could have been given as a concert work. Whatever Monteverdi's intention in publishing the collection, he can only have had a liturgical context in mind for its performance. Re-creating a liturgy on a gramophone recording is a little difficult, since liturgy involves action as well as sound. In this respect, though, Vespers is easier to portray than a Mass. The interpolated liturgical texts are generally rather short, and any celebration of Vespers which uses polyphony gives the impression of a concert-like sequence of music running from the introductory rite to the end of the Magnificat. From the Magnificat to the end of Vespers, however, the dynamics of a liturgical performance are rather different from those of a concert performance. After the climax represented by the Magnificat, with the ritual censing of the altar, and the playing of the 'Sonata sopra Sancta Maria' (if we accept that this should be its correct liturgical position), Vespers gradually subsides into contemplation and prayer, though there is still more music to be heard in the Marian devotions which conclude the service. In church, a quiet, devotional conclusion seems wholly appropriate; in the concert hall it is apt to disappoint those who feel that the performance of such a grand conception as the music of the 1610 Vespers should end in some sort of musical climax.

A liturgical performance should, nonetheless, form the starting point for any exploration of the 1610 Vespers on record. Only two such performances are available; the experimental *Vespers of Santa Barbara*, directed by Harry Christophers (1989), which is a reconstruction of the original context for which Monteverdi might have written the music – Second Vespers for the patronal festival of the ducal chapel at Mantua. This involves several changes to the music as published, including substitution of a different hymn (though 'Ave maris stella' is added as an appendix on the CDs) and the substitution of the phrase 'Sancta Barbara ora pro nobis' for 'Sancta Maria ora pro nobis' in the 'Sonata sopra Sancta Maria'. Whatever the merits of the hypothesis that Monteverdi might have written most of the 1610 Vespers music for performance at Santa Barbara, Mantua, the substituted text in the Sonata does not fit as well as the original.

The other liturgical reconstruction, this time for a Marian feast – Second Vespers for the Feast of the Assumption (15 August) – is found on the 1984 recording directed by Andrew Parrott. This recording, which stemmed from a performance that Parrott had directed for a BBC Promenade Concert in 1977, was, like Jürgens's 1966/67 recording, a landmark in Vespers interpretations. In addition to the liturgical context that it re-creates, the full choir is restricted to those items where its use seems most appropriate, there is no instrumental doubling except where indicated by Monteverdi, and it was the first recording in which the 'Lauda Ierusalem' and Magnificat were transposed down a fourth.

The most striking change in the decade since Parrott's recording was made is the use of faster tempi, as illustrated on a recording such as Philip Pickett's excellent semi-liturgical performance of 1991, which also represents a performance in which plainsong antiphons are sung both before and after the psalms and Magnificat. As was suggested above, however, ideas about how the 1610 Vespers should be performed are still to some extent in a state of flux, and there is ample room for new interpretations. And personal taste will, no doubt, continue to play a large part in the choice of a favourite recording. As one reviewer put it in 1991: 'it would be easy to argue that the best record of the Monteverdi Vespers is one of the earliest, that conducted by Anthony Lewis – vivacious, exciting, teeming with conviction and above all constantly dancing'.[29]

Appendix 1

Second Vespers for the Feast of the Assumption of the Blessed Virgin (15 August)

The Latin versions of the texts given below are taken from the *Breviarium Romanum* (Venice, 1598). The English versions are from Lefebvre, *Saint Andrew Daily Missal*. For the full texts of the psalms, hymn and Magnificat, see Appendix 2. On the difference between the Vulgate and the Book of Common Prayer (BCP) numberings of the psalms see Chapter 2, n. 3.

Versicle [V]:	*Deus in adiutorium meum intende.*	O God, come to my assistance.	Intonation formula: see Appendix 2, below, p. 105; *LU*, p. 250).
Response [R]:	*Domine ad adiuvandum me festina.*	O Lord, make haste to help me.	
Doxology:	*Gloria patri, et filio: et spiritui sancto. Sicut erat in principio et nunc et semper: et in secula seculorum. Amen.*	Glory be to the Father, and to the Son, and to the Holy Ghost. As it was in the beginning, is now and ever shall be, world without end. Amen.	
Alleluia:	*Alleluia.*	Alleluia.	
Antiphon:	*Assumpta est Maria in cœlum: gaudent Angeli, laudantes benedicunt Dominum.*	Mary has been taken up into heaven, the angels rejoice, and bless God with songs of praise.	Composed plainsong, Mode 7 (*LU*, p. 1605).
Psalm 109 (BCP 110): *Dixit Dominus*	Psalm 109 (110)		Psalm Tone 7, termination a (*LU*, p. 116; with psalm text, pp. 132–3).
Antiphon:	*Assumpta est Maria in cœlum …*	Mary has been taken up into heaven: …	Composed plainsong repeated.

Antiphon:	*Maria virgo assumpta est ad æthereum thalamum: in quo rex regum stellato sedet solio.*	*The Virgin Mary has been taken into the bridal-chamber of heaven, where the King of kings sitteth on a throne amid the stars.*	Composed plainsong Mode 8 (*LU*, pp. 1605–6).
Psalm 112 (BCP 113): *Laudate pueri*		Psalm 112 (113)	Psalm Tone 8, termination G (*LU*, p. 117; with psalm text, p. 152).
Antiphon:	*Maria virgo assumpta est …*	*The Virgin Mary …*	Composed plainsong repeated.
Antiphon:	*In odorem unguentorum tuorum currimus, adolescentulæ dilexerunt te nimis.*	*We run on the scent of thine ointments: the young maidens love thee exceedingly.*	Composed plainsong Mode 4 (*LU*, p. 1606).
Psalm 121 (BCP 122): *Lætatus sum*		Psalm 121 (122)	Psalm Tone 4, termination A* (*LU*, p. 115; with psalm text, pp. 171–2).
Antiphon:	*In odorem unguentorum …*	*We run on the scent …*	Composed plainsong repeated.
Antiphon:	*Benedicta filia tu à Domino, quia per te fructum vitæ communicavimus.*	*O daughter, blessed art thou of the Lord: for through thee we have partaken of the fruit of life.*	Composed plainsong Mode 7 (*LU*, p. 1606).
Psalm 126 (BCP 127): *Nisi Dominus*		Psalm 126 (127)	Psalm Tone 7, termination c2 (*LU*, p. 116; with psalm text, pp. 176–7).
Antiphon:	*Benedicta filia tua …*	*O daughter, blessed art thou …*	Composed plainsong repeated.

Antiphon:	*Pulchra es et decora filia Ierusalem, terribilis ut castrorum acies ordinata.*	*Fair and beautiful art thou, O daughter of Jerusalem, terrible as an army in battle array.*	Composed plainsong Mode 1 (*LU*, p. 1606).
Psalm 147 (BCP 147, vv 12–20): *Lauda Ierusalem*		Psalm 147 (147, vv 12–20)	Psalm Tone 1, termination g2 (*LU*, p. 113; with psalm text, pp. 202–3).
Antiphon:	*Pulchra es, et decora …*	*Fair and beautiful art thou …*	Composed plainsong repeated.
Chapter (Ecclesiastes 24): *In omnibus requiem quæsivi, et in hæreditate domini morabor: tunc præcipit, et dixit mihi creator omnium: et qui creavit me, requievit in tabernaculo meo.*		*In all things I sought for rest, and in the inheritance of the Lord shall I abide: so the Creator of all things gave me a commandment, and He that made me rested within my tabernacle.*	Formula (*LU*, p. 123).
R:	*Deo gratias.*	*Thanks be to God.*	
Hymn:	*Ave maris stella*	Hymn	Composed plainsong, see below, Appendix 2, p. 116–17 (for another version of the melody, see *LU*, p. 1259)
V:	*Exaltata est sancta Dei genitrix.*	*The holy Mother of God is lifted up on high.*	Composed plainsong (*LU*, p. 1607).
R:	*Super choros angelorum ad cælestia regna.*	*Above the choirs of angels into the kingdom of heaven.*	

Antiphon:	Hodie Maria virgo cælos ascendit, gaude-te, quia cum Christo regnat in æternum.	This day the Virgin Mary ascended into heaven: rejoice, for she reigns with Christ for ever.	Composed plainsong Mode 8 (*LU*, p. 1607).
Magnificat		Magnificat	Magnificat Tone 8, termination G (with text, *LU*, p. 212; a more or-nate Magnificat tone for use on Doubles of the First Class is given on p. 218).
Antiphon:	Hodie Maria Virgo …	This day the Virgin Mary …	Composed plainsong repeated.
V:	Dominus vobiscum.	The Lord be with you.	Formula (*LU*, p. 98).
R:	Et cum spritu tuo.	And with thy spirit.	
Collect (Prayer):	Oremus. Famulorum tuorum, quæsumus domine, delictis ignosce: ut qui tibi placere de actibus nostris non valemus, genitricis filii tui domini nostri intercessione salve-mur. Per eundem Dominum nostrum Iesum Christum filium tuum, qui tecum vivit et regnat in unitate Spiritus sancti, Deus: per omnia sæcula saeculorum.	Let us pray. We beseech Thee, O Lord, to forgive the sins of Thy servants: that since by our own acts we are not worthy to please Thee, yet by the intercession of Thy Son, Jesus Christ our Lord, we may be saved. Through the same our Lord Jesus Christ, Thy Son, who is God, and liveth and reign-eth with Thee in the unity of the Holy Ghost: world without end.	
R:	Amen.	Amen.	

V:	Dominus vobiscum.	The Lord be with you.	Formula (*LU*, p. 98 or p. 100).
R:	Et cum spiritu tuo.	And with thy spirit.	
V:	Benedicamus domino.	Let us bless the Lord.	Version for Feasts of the Blessed Virgin (*LU*, p. 126).
R:	Deo gratias.	Thanks be to God.	

Appendix 2

Plainsongs, texts and translations

This Appendix contains the texts, with translations, of all the items that Monteverdi published under the heading 'Vespro della B[eata] Vergine' in his 1610 print, together with plainsongs for the versicle and response, the psalms, hymn, sonata and Magnificat. In the case of this latter group, the texts and plainsongs represent an attempt to establish as nearly as possible the raw materials with which Monteverdi worked. A fundamental problem for both historians and analysts is that we do not know on which liturgical sources Monteverdi drew for his texts and plainsongs. One thing is certain, however: that *LU*, which is so often used in analyses of the 1610 Vespers, is an unsuitable starting point for such endeavours.

A comparison between the readings of the 1610 print and modern compilations of liturgical texts and plainsongs such as *LU* and the *Antiphonale Monasticum* (henceforth *AM*) reveals a number of small, but interesting variants. An obvious question that these raise is whether they represent standard Roman usage in the late sixteenth and early seventeenth centuries, or whether Monteverdi was working from a local use, such as that of the ducal church of Santa Barbara in Mantua.

The variants are:

(1) 'Dixit Dominus', verse 4: in Monteverdi's setting (bar 52 (Bt 100)) the first part of the verse ends after 'virtutis tuae' and not after 'in splendoribus sanctorum';

(2) 'Lætatus sum', verse 4: in Monteverdi's setting (bars 42–3 (Bt 73–6; St 41–2)) the first part of the verse ends after 'testimonium Israel' rather than after 'tribus Domini';

(3) 'Dixit Dominus', verse 8: all but one of the part-books have 'bibit' instead of 'bibet' (the final syllable is missing in the Bassus part); further, while the A, T, B, Q and S part-books have 'exaltabit', the Cantus part has 'exaltavit'.

(4) 'Ave maris stella', verse 7, line 4: six of the seven part-books have 'Trinus' instead of 'Tribus' (the word is indistinct in the Quintus part);

(5) In the 1610 print the words 'dominus' (/ 'dominum' / 'domini', etc.) almost always, and 'spiritui sancto' always, appear with a lower-case initial letter unless at the beginning of a line, while 'Deus' (/ 'Dei' / 'Deum'), 'Patri', 'Filio' are consistently given an initial capital. In *LU* all these words are given initial capitals.

These readings have been compared with those found in five late sixteenth- and early seventeenth-century Italian sources representing both the Roman use and the local use of the ducal church of Santa Barbara, Mantua:

(a) *Breviarium Romanum* (Venice, 1598)
(b) *Breviarium Romanum* (Venice, 1603)
(c) *Psalterium Chorale* (Venice, 1585)
(d) *Breviarii S. Barbarae* (Venice, 1583): the breviary of the Santa Barbara, Mantua, usage.
(e) Mantua, Archivio storico diocesano, Fondo Basilica ex Palatino di Santa Barbara, MS 18 [part of the Santa Barbara Ferial Psalter], ff. xl^v ('Dixit Dominus'), lvij^r ('Lætatus sum'), MS 9 [Proprium sanctorum, December–June], f. 48^v.

None of these sources provides a wholly satisfactory explanation for variant (1). Sources (a) and (b) correspond to the usage of the *LU* and *AM*: that is, they have no punctuation after 'virtutis tuae', but have a colon – the standard indication for the internal division of the verse – after 'in splendoribus sanctorum'. Source (d) has a comma after 'virtutis tuae' and a colon after 'in splendoribus sanctorum'. Source (e) has a colon surmounted by an oblique (⸫) after 'virtutis tuae' and a colon after 'in splendoribus sanctorum'. And source (c) has a narrow oblique after 'virtutis tuae' and a colon after 'in splendoribus sanctorum'. Sources (c), (d) and (e) are, therefore, punctuated after 'virtutis tuae' though in each case the symbol used is either a comma or the equivalent of a comma.

Variant (2) can be resolved more satisfactorily. Only source (b) has a colon after 'tribus domini', and no punctuation after 'testimonium Israel'. Source (c) has a colon at both junctures. Sources (d) and (e) have a comma and comma surmounted by oblique, respectively, after 'tribus domini', and a full colon only after 'testimonium Israel'. Source (a) has no punctuation after 'tribus domini', but a colon after 'testimonium Israel' – corresponding exactly to Monteverdi's usage.

Variant (3): only source (b) has the reading 'bibet'. All the others have 'bibit' and sources (a) and (d) also have 'exaltavit'.
Variant (4): none of the sources has the reading 'Trinus'.
Variant (5): sources (a), (d) and (e) correspond to Monteverdi's usage.

In respect of these variants, then, sources (d) and (e) – the Santa Barbara breviary and Ferial Psalter – have the largest number of correspondences with Monteverdi's usage, followed very closely by source (a) – the Tridentine breviary of 1598: that is, both a standard Roman source and the Santa Barbara books sanction most of the variants found in Monteverdi's print. Only the Tridentine breviary of 1603 has no correspondences at all: it conforms to the usage found in *LU* and *AM*. Since the Tridentine books available for the present study constitute only a random sample, since none of the volumes consulted sanction variant (4), and since Monteverdi does not follow the Santa Barbara books in, for example, spelling 'Ierusalem' as 'Hierusalem', it would be dangerous to draw from this evidence any conclusions about the precise liturgical sources on which he drew for his texts. What we can say, however, is that the variants in his texts are found in both standard Roman and Santa Barbara usages and in this respect at least his settings would have been usable in either context.

With the exception of Tone 1, for the Magnificat, the psalm tones reproduced in this Appendix are those appointed for double feasts in Giovanni Guidetti's *Directorium Chori*, revised by Giovanni Francisco Massano (Rome, 1604), pp. 560–3. (The version of Tone 1 used by Monteverdi is simpler than that given for double feasts in the *Directorium*.) Comparison of the final cadence formulae in this Roman source with those found in the Santa Barbara *Commune Sanctorum* and Ferial Psalter (Mantua, Archivio storico diocesano, Fondo Basilica ex Palatino di Santa Barbara, MSS 15 and 18 respectively) shows that in both melodic outline and the placement of ligatures (indicated in the transcriptions below by the use of slurs) the two uses correspond exactly.[1] Monteverdi's use of patterns of text underlay which cut across the ligatures (in 'Lauda Ierusalem' and the two Magnificat settings) cannot, therefore, be attributed to his having used a Santa Barbara rather than a Roman source or vice versa. The divergences may simply represent compositional decisions, though they may also owe something to a contemporary performance practice with which Monteverdi was familiar. This certainly seems to be the case with regard to the pitches that Monteverdi chooses to accommodate extra unaccented syllables following the last main accent in each of the first and second parts of the verse in 'Dixit Dominus', 'Laudate pueri', 'Lætatus sum', 'Lauda Ierusalem' and the Magnificat settings (the void semibreves in the plainsongs given below). In these, his usage differs from that suggested in *LU*. In the first half-verse in 'Lauda Ierusalem' he also consistently omits the second note of the ligature except where it is needed

---

[1] There seems to be no surviving Tonary for the Santa Barbara use. It has been impossible, therefore, to compare the opening and median formulae of the Santa Barbara psalm tones with those of Roman usage.

Example 15(a)

Di - xit__ Do - mi-nus Do - mi - no me - o: Se - de a dex-tris me - is.

Example 15(b)

Glo - ri - a Pa - tri, et Fi - li - o: et spi - ri - tu - i sanc-to. Si - cut e - rat in prin - ci - pi - o

et nunc et sem - per:__ et in se - cu - la se - cu-lo-rum. A - men.__

for unaccented syllables (see, for example, bar 3 of his setting (Bt 5)) and this has been reflected in the presentation of the plainsong below. On the versions of the 'Ave maris stella' melody, see the discussion in Chapter 3, above, pp. 33–4.

Although the plainsongs are shown below in a notation which suggests that they are to be sung in notes of equal length, Guidetti's *Directorium Chori*, compiled for priests rather than musicians, in fact prescribes a simple rhythmic interpretation, with three note values – the long (value $1\frac{1}{2}$ units), the breve (value 1) and the semibreve (value $\frac{1}{2}$). If we represent the breve as a crotchet, then Psalm Tone 4 as shown in the *Directorium* would appear as in Example 15(a) and the initial versicle as shown below, p. 105 (the choral response is not given in the 1604 edition of the *Directorium*). A more extended example of this rhythmic notation is shown as Example 15(b); this is the doxology of one of the versions of the psalm 'Venite exultemus Domino' printed in full in the *Directorium*.[2] If rhythmic interpretation of plainsong notation was, indeed, widespread in early seventeenth-century Italy, then the rhythmicisations used by Monteverdi in the psalm, hymn and Magnificat settings of the 1610 Vespers may owe something, in principle at least, to this usage.[3] This is, however, an area which still has to be investigated fully, and it should be said that the notation of the Santa Barbara plainsong repertory is by no means as simple to interpret as that of the *Directorium Chori*.

In the versions of the texts given below I have generally followed the spelling and use of capital letters found in Monteverdi's 1610 print except

[2] *Directorium Chori*, 540–1.

[3] I am very grateful to Graham Dixon for reminding me of the potential importance of the rhythmic interpretation of plainsong in the *Directorium Chori*.

that the double i form 'ij' has been modernised to 'ii', the letter u changed to v where appropriate and ampersands changed to 'et'. The contraction ę, which is regularly used as a substitute for both 'æ' and 'œ', has been expanded into the corresponding ligature (both are pronounced as though they were the single Italian vowel 'e').[4] In Monteverdi's print 'secula' and 'seculorum' (and 'seculum') are always spelled in this form, and never 'saecula' and 'saeculorum' as in more recent Latin liturgical books.

The 1610 print is sparsely and inconsistently punctuated. In providing a fully punctuated text of the versicle and response, psalms, hymn and Magnificat I have been guided by the usage of the *Breviarium Romanum* (Venice, 1598). Italics and underlining in the texts, and accents in the music are editorial and are intended as a guide to chanting the psalms (see above, Chapter 2). English versions of these texts are from Lefebvre, *Saint Andrew Daily Missal*, pp. 968, 970, 974–5, 984, 998–1000, 1005 and differ from those given in the Book of Common Prayer. In the case of the sacred concertos, the texts of which are compilations ('Nigra sum', 'Pulchra es', 'Duo Seraphim') or of unidentified authorship ('Audi cœlum'), punctuation is editorial. The translations of 'Nigra sum' and 'Pulchra es' are adapted from the translation of *The Song of Songs* in E. Ann Matter, *The Voice of My Beloved: the Song of Songs in Western Medieval Christianity* (Philadelphia, 1990), pp. xvi–xix and xxviii–xxix respectively. The translation of 'Audi cœlum' is that given in Monteverdi, *Vespro della Beata Vergine*, ed. Jerome Roche, pp. 248–50.

---

[4] The three forms 'hereditas', 'hęreditas' and 'hæreditas' are all used in the underlay of the fourth verse of 'Nisi Dominus', and 'celum', 'cęlum' and 'cœlum' in the first line of 'Audi cœlum'. Occasionally the contraction and the corresponding ligature are used almost simultaneously in different voices.

Versicle and response

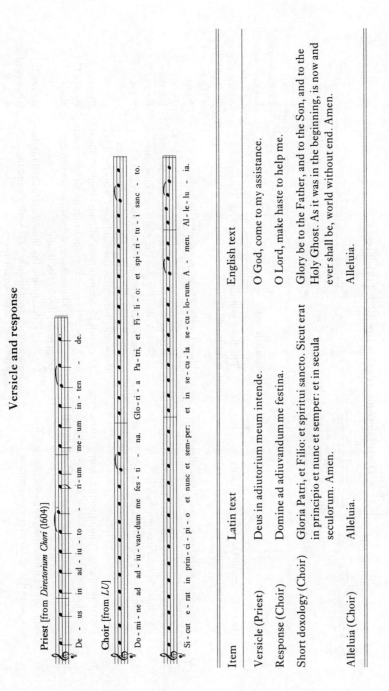

Priest [from *Directorium Chori* (1604)]

De - us in ad - iu - to - ri - um me - um in - ten - de.

Choir [from *LU*]

Do - mi - ne ad ad - iu - van - dum me fes - ti - na. Glo - ri - a Pa - tri, et Fi - li - o: et spi - ri - tu - i sanc - to.

Si - cut e - rat in prin - ci - pi - o et nunc et sem - per: et in se - cu - la se - cu - lo - rum. A - men. Al - le - lu - ia.

Item	Latin text	English text
Versicle (Priest)	Deus in adiutorium meum intende.	O God, come to my assistance.
Response (Choir)	Domine ad adiuvandum me festina.	O Lord, make haste to help me.
Short doxology (Choir)	Gloria Patri, et Filio: et spiritui sancto. Sicut erat in principio et nunc et semper: et in secula seculorum. Amen.	Glory be to the Father, and to the Son, and to the Holy Ghost. As it was in the beginning, is now and ever shall be, world without end. Amen.
Alleluia (Choir)	Alleluia.	Alleluia.

Dixit Dominus (Psalm 109; BCP 110). Tone 4.

Di - xit —— Dominus Do - mi - no meo: * sede a dex - tris me - is.
Donec ponam ini- mi - cos tu - os: * scabellum pe - dum tu - o - rum.

Verse	Latin text	English text	Part(s) bearing cantus firmus
1.	Dixit Dominus Domino meo: * sede a dextris meis.	The Lord said unto my Lord: * Sit Thou at my right hand.	S (first phrase anticipated in T, Q, B)
2.	Donec ponam inimicos tuos: * scabellum pedum tuorum.	Until I make Thine enemies * Thy footstool.	None
3.	Virgam virtutis tuae emittet dominus ex Sion: * dominare in medio inimicorum tuorum.	The Lord shall send the rod of Thy strength out of Sion: * rule Thou in the midst of Thine enemies.	Bg, then Bg and B
4.	Tecum principium in die virtutis tuæ[5] * in splendoribus sanctorum: ex utero ante luciferum genui te.	Thine shall be the dominion in the day of Thy power, * amid the brightness of the saints: from the womb, before the daystar have I begotten Thee.	None
5.	Iuravit dominus, et non pœnitebit eum: * tu es sacerdos in æternum secundum ordinem Melchisedech.	The Lord hath sworn, and will not repent: * Thou art a Priest for ever after the order of Melchisedech.	Bg, then Bg and B
6.	Dominus a dextris tuis: * confregit in die iræ suæ Reges.	The Lord at Thy right hand * shall strike through kings in the day of His wrath.	None
7.	Iudicabit in nationibus, implebit ruinas: * conquassabit capita in terra multorum.	He shall judge among the heathen, He shall fill the places with dead bodies: * He shall wound the heads over many countries.	Bg and B (shadowed in T, A, S, C)

8.	De torrente in *via* bibit: * propterea ex*altavit* caput.	He shall drink of the brook in the way: * therefore shall he lift up his head.	None
9.	Gloria P*atri, et* F*ilio:* * et sp*iritui* sancto.	Glory be to the Father, and to the Son, * and to the Holy Ghost.	T
10.	Sicut erat in principio, et *nunc, et* s*emper:* * et in secula sec*ulorum.* Amen.	As it was in the beginning, is now, and ever shall be, * world without end. Amen.	B C

Note: ⁵ On the division of the verse at this point see the discussion of textual variants above, pp. 100–101.

Nigra sum

Nigra sum sed formosa filiæ Ierusalem.	I am black but beautiful, daughters of Jerusalem.
Ideo dilexit me Rex et introduxit	Therefore the king has loved me and brought me
in cubiculum suum et dixit mihi:	into his chamber, and said to me:
surge, amica mea, et veni	rise, my friend, and come,
iam hiems transiit	for now the winter has passed;
imber abiit et recessit	the rain has gone and departed;
flores apparuerunt in terra nostra	flowers appear in our land;
tempus putationis advenit.	the time of pruning has come.

Note: Translation from E. Ann Matter, *The Voice of My Beloved: The Song of Songs in Western Medieval Christianity.* Copyright 1990 by the University of Pennsylvania Press. Reprinted with permission of the University of Pennsylvania Press. From The Song of Songs, verses 1:4, 1:3, 2:10–2:12.

Laudate pueri Dominum (Psalm 112; BCP 113). Tone 8.

Lau - da - te pueri do - mi - num: * laudate no - men do - mi - ni.
Sit nomen domini bene-dic - - tum: * ex hoc nunc, et us-que in se - cu - lum.

Verse	Latin text	English text	Part(s) bearing *cantus firmus*
1.	Laudate pueri dominum: * laudate *nomen* domini.	Praise the Lord, O ye His servants: * praise the name of the Lord.	Q, T, Bl, C
2.	Sit nomen domini benedictum: * ex hoc, nunc, et *usque in* seculum.	Blessed be the name of the Lord: * from this time forth, and for evermore.	Q
3.	A solis ortu usque ad occasum: * laudabile *nomen* domini.	From the rising of the sun unto the going down of the same, * the name of the Lord is to be praised.	A
4.	Excelsus super omnes gentes dominus: * et super cœlos *gloria* eius.	The Lord is high above all nations, * and His glory above the heavens.	C
5.	Quis sicut dominus Deus noster, qui in altis habitat: * et humilia respicit in cœlo, *et in* terra.	Who is like unto the Lord our God, who dwelleth on high, * and beholdeth what is lowly in heaven and in the earth?	S
6.	Suscitans a terra inopem: * et de stercore *erigens* pauperem.	He raiseth up the poor out of the dust, * and lifteth the needy out of the dung-hill:	A
7.	Ut collocet eum cum principibus: * cum principibus *populi* sui.	That he may set him with princes, * even with the princes of His people.	Q

8.	Qui habitare facit sterilem in *do*mo: * matrem filio*rum læ*tantem.	He maketh the barren woman to keep house, * and to be a joyful mother of children.	T
9.	Gloria Patri, et *Fi*lio: * et spir*itui* sancto.	Glory be to the Father, and to the Son, * and to the Holy Ghost.	Q
10.	Sicut erat in principio, et nunc, et *sem*per: * et in secula secu*lorum*. *A*men.	As it was in the beginning, is now, and ever shall be, * world without end. Amen.	Q (first phrase also in C; second phrase also in T, BII)

Pulchra es

Pulchra es amica mea suavis et decora filia Ierusalem.
Pulchra es amica mea suavis et decora sicut Ierusalem
terribilis ut castrorum acies ordinata.
Averte oculos tuos a me quia ipsi me avolare fecerunt.

You are fair, my friend, sweet and beautiful daughter of Jerusalem.
You are fair, my friend, sweet and beautiful like Jerusalem,
terrible as a battle line drawn up from camps.
Turn away your eyes from me, for they make me flee.

Note: Translation from E. Ann Matter, *The Voice of My Beloved: The Song of Songs in Western Medieval Christianity.* Copyright 1990 by the University of Pennsylvania Press. Reprinted with permission of the University of Pennsylvania Press. From The Song of Songs, verses 6:3–6:4.

Lætatus sum (Psalm 121; BCP 122). Tone 2.

Chant: Læ - ta - tus sum in his quæ dicta sunt mi - hi: * in domum domi-ni i - bi - mus.
Stantes erant pedes no - stri: * in atriis tuis Ie - ru - sa - lem.

Verse	Latin text	English text	Part(s) bearing *cantus firmus*
1.	Lætatus sum in his, quæ dicta sunt mihi: * in domum domini ibimus.	I was glad when they said unto me: * Let us go into the house of the Lord.	T
2.	Stantes erant pedes nostri: * in atriis tuis Ierusalem.	Our feet have been wont to stand * within thy gates, O Jerusalem.	None
3.	Ierusalem, quæ ædificatur ut civitas: * cuius participatio eius in idipsum.	Jerusalem is builded as a city * that is compact together:	None
4.	Illuc enim ascenderunt tribus tribus Domini testimonium Israel:[6] * ad confitendum nomini domini.	Whither the tribes go up, the tribes of the Lord, the testimony of Israel, * to give thanks unto the name of the Lord.	C
5.	Quia illic sederunt sedes in iudicio: * sedes super domum David.	For there are set thrones for judgment, * the thrones for the house of David.	A then C
6.	Rogate quæ ad pacem sunt Ierusalem: * et abundantia diligentibus te.[7]	Pray for the peace of Jerusalem: * they shall prosper that love thee.	None
7.	Fiat pax in virtute tua: * et abundantia in turribus tuis.	Peace be within thy walls, * and prosperity within thy palaces.	C

#		English	
8.	Propter fratres meos, et proximos meos: *	For my brethren and companions' sakes, *	S
	loquebar pacem de te.	I will now say: Peace be within thee.	A then S
9.	Propter domum domini Dei nostri: * quæsivi bona tibi.	Because of the house of the Lord our God, * I will seek thy good.	None
10.	Gloria Patri, et Filio: * et spiritui sancto.	Glory be to the Father, and to the Son, * and to the Holy Ghost.	None
11.	Sicut erat in principio, et nunc, et semper: *	As it was in the beginning, is now,	C
	et in secula seculorum. Amen.	and ever shall be, * world without end. Amen.	A then S

Note: [6] On the division of the verse at this point see the discussion of textual variants above, pp. 100–101.

[7] On the use of accents in this verse and verse 8, see above, Chapter 2, note 10.

Duo Seraphim

Duo Seraphim clamabant alter ad alterum:	Two Seraphim cried one to the other:
Sanctus, sanctus, sanctus Dominus Deus Sabaoth.	Holy, holy, holy, Lord God of hosts.
Plena est omnis terra gloria eius.	The whole earth is full of His glory.
Tres sunt qui testimonium dant in cœlo	There are three that bear witness in heaven:
Pater, Verbum, et Spiritus Sanctus.	the Father, the Word and the Holy Ghost.
Et hi tres unum sunt.	And these three are one.
Sanctus, sanctus, sanctus Dominus Deus Sabaoth.	Holy, holy, holy, Lord God of hosts.
Plena est omnis terra gloria eius.	The whole earth is full of His glory.

Nisi Dominus (Psalm 126; BCP 127). Tone 6.

Ni - si —— dominus ædificave - *rit* do - ta - mum: * in vanum laboraverunt, qui ædi - *fi* - *cant* —— e - am.

Nisi dominus custodierit ci - *vi* - ta - tem: * frustra vigilat qui cus to - *dit* —— e - am.

Verse	Latin text	English text	Part(s) bearing *cantus firmus*
1.	Nisi dominus ædificaverit *domum*: * in vanum laboraverunt, qui ædi*ficant* eam.	Except the Lord build the house, * they labour in vain that build it.	T1 and Q2
2.	Nisi dominus custodierit ci*vitatem*: * frustra vigilat, qui cus*todit* eam.	Except the Lord keep the city, * the watchman waketh but in vain.	T1 then Q2
3.	Vanum est vobis ante lu*cem* surgere: * surgite postquam sederitis, qui manducatis pa*nem dolo*ris.	It is vain for you to rise up early, * rise up when ye are rested, ye that eat the bread of sorrow.	T1 then Q2
4.	Cum dederit dilectis suis *sommum*: * ecce hæreditas domini filii merces *fructus ven*tris.	For He giveth his beloved sleep: * Lo, children are an heritage of the Lord: the fruit of the womb is His reward.	T1 then Q2
5.	Sicut sagittæ in manu *potentis*: * ita filii *excussorum*.	As arrows are in the hand of a mighty man, * so are the children of the outcast.	T1 then Q2
6.	Beatus vir, qui implevit desiderium suum *ex ipsis*: * non confundetur cum loquetur inimicis suis *in porta*.	Happy is the man that hath his desire satisfied with them: * he shall not be confounded when he speaketh with his enemies in the gate.	T1 then T1 and Q2

7. Gloria Patri, *et* Filio: * et spir*itui* sancto.

   Glory be to the Father, and to the Son, * and to the Holy Ghost.   T1 and Q2

8. Sicut erat in principio, et nunc, *et* semper: * et in secula secul*orum*. Amen.

   As it was in the beginning, is now, and ever shall be, * world without end. Amen.   T1 and Q2

Audi cœlum

Audi cœlum verba mea plena desiderio et perfusa gaudio.
Echo: Audio.

Hear, O heaven, my words full of longing and suffused with joy.
Echo: I hear.

Dic quæso mihi: quæ est ista quæ consurgens ut aurora rutilat, et benedicam?
Echo: Dicam.

I beseech you, tell me who is she that rises up, bright as the dawn, and I shall bless her?
Echo: I shall tell you.

Dic nam ista pulchra ut luna electa ut sol replet lætitia terras, cœlos maria?
Echo: Maria.

Say if this lady, lovely as the moon and glorious as the sun, fills with gladness the earth, heavens and seas?
Echo: Mary.

Maria virgo illa dulcis prædicata a Prophetis Ezechiel porta Orientalis?
Echo: Talis.

That sweet virgin Mary, foretold by the prophet Ezekiel, that eastern gate?
Echo: The same!

Illa sacra et fœlix porta per quam mors fuit expulsa introduxit autem vita?
Echo: Ita.

that sacred and joyful portal through which death was expelled and life renewed?
Echo: Thus!

Quæ semper tutum est medium inter hominem et Deum pro culpis remedium?
Echo: Medium.

Omnes hanc ergo sequamur qua cum gratia mereamur vitam æternam consequamur.
Echo: Sequamur.

Præstet nobis Deus Pater hoc et filius et mater cuius nomen invocamus dulce miseris solamen.
Echo: Amen.

Benedicta es virgo Maria in seculorum secula.

who is always a trusted mediator between God and man, for the for-giveness of sins?
Echo: a mediator.

Let us all therefore follow her, through whom we may with grace deserve to attain life everlasting.
Echo: May we follow.

May God the Father, and the Son, and the mother whose sweet name we invoke, grant solace to the afflicted.
Echo: Amen.

Blessed art thou, virgin Mary, for ever and ever.

Note: Translation by Jerome Roche © Ernst Eulenburg Ltd, London. Reprinted by permission.

Lauda Ierusalem (Psalm 147; BCP 147, vv 12-20). Tone 3.

Lau-da Ie - - - - - - ru - sa - lem do - mi - num: * lauda Deum tu - um Si - on.___

Quoniam confortavit seras por- ta - rum tu - a - rum: * benedixit filiis tu - is in___ te.___

Verse	Latin text	English text	Part(s) bearing cantus firmus
1.	Lauda Ierusalem dominum: * lauda Deum tuum Sion.[8]	Praise the Lord, O Jerusalem: * praise thy God, O Sion.	T
2.	Quoniam confortavit seras portarum tuarum: * benedixit filiis tuis in te.	For He hath strengthened the bars of thy gates: * He hath blessed thy children within thee.	T
3.	Qui posuit fines tuos pacem: * et adipe frumenti satiat te.	He maketh peace in thy borders: * and filleth thee with the finest of the wheat.	T
4.	Qui emittet eloquium suum terræ: * velociter currit sermo eius.	He sendeth forth His commandment upon earth: His word runneth very swiftly.	T
5.	Qui dat nivem sicut lanam: * nebulam sicut cinerem spargit.	He giveth snow like wool: * He scattereth the hoarfrost like ashes.	T
6.	Mittit cristallum suam sicut bucellas [sic]: * ante faciem frigoris eius quis sustinebit?	He casteth forth His ice like morsels: * who can stand before His cold?	T
7.	Emittet verbum suum, et liquefaciet ea: * flabit spiritus eius, et fluent aquæ.	He sendeth out His word, and melteth them: * He causeth His wind to blow, and the waters flow.	T
8.	Qui annunciat verbum suum Iacob: * iustitias, et iudicia sua Israel.	He declareth His word unto Jacob, * His statutes and His judgements unto Israel.	T
9.	Non fecit taliter omni nationi: * et iudicia sua non manifestavit eis.	He hath not dealt so with all nations: * neither hath He made known to them His judgements.	T
10.	Gloria Patri, et Filio: * et spiritui sancto.	Glory be to the Father, and to the Son, * and to the Holy Ghost.	C
11.	Sicut erat in principio, et nunc, et semper: * et in secula seculorum. Amen.	As it was in the beginning, is now, and ever shall be, * world without end. Amen.	S, then S & C S B, then Q & S

Note: [8] On the use of accents in this psalm, see above, Chapter 2, note 10.

Sonata sopra Sancta Maria

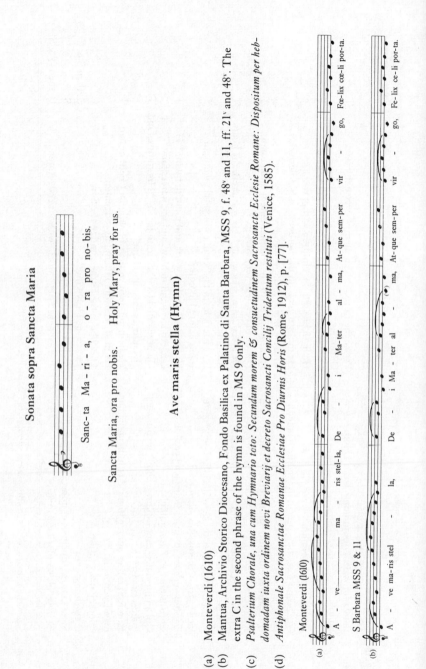

Sanc-ta Ma - ri - a, o - ra pro no - bis.

Sancta Maria, ora pro nobis.   Holy Mary, pray for us.

Ave maris stella (Hymn)

(a) Monteverdi (1610)

(b) Mantua, Archivio Storico Diocesano, Fondo Basilica ex Palatino di Santa Barbara, MSS 9, f. 48ᵛ and 11, ff. 21ᵛ and 48ᵛ. The extra C in the second phrase of the hymn is found in MS 9 only.

(c) *Psalterium Chorale, una cum Hymnario toto: Secundum morem & consuetudinem Sacrosancte Ecclesie Romane: Dispositum per hebdomadam iuxta ordinem novi Breviarij et decreto Sacrosancti Concilij Tridentum restituti* (Venice, 1585).

(d) *Antiphonale Sacrosanctae Romanae Ecclesiae Pro Diurnis Horis* (Rome, 1912), p. [77].

Monteverdi (1610)

(a)
A - ve——— ma - ris stel-la, De - i Ma-ter al - ma, At-que sem-per vir - go, Foe-lix cœ-li por-ta.

S Barbara MSS 9 & 11

(b)
A - ve ma-ris stel - la, De - i Ma - ter al - ma, At-que sem-per vir - go, Fe-lix cœ-li por-ta.

Psalterium (1585)

(c) A - ve _ ma-ris _ stel - la De - i Ma - ter al - ma, At-que sem-per vir - go, _ Fe-lix cæ-li por-ta.

Antiphonale (1912)

(d) A - ve _ ma-ris _ stel-la, _ De - i Ma - ter al - ma, At-que sem-per vir-go, _ Fe-lix cœ-li por-ta.

Verse	Latin text	English text
1.	Ave maris stella,	Hail, star of the sea,
	Dei Mater alma,	mother of God
	Atque semper virgo,	and ever virgin,
	Fœlix cœli porta.	joyful gate of heaven.
2.	Sumens illud ave	Receiving that 'Ave'
	Gabrielis ore,	spoken by Gabriel
	Funda nos in pace,	and reversing the name 'Eva',
	Mutans Evæ nomen.	establish peace in our lives.
3.	Solve vincla reis,	Loose the bonds of sin,
	Profer lumen cæcis,	bring light to the blind,
	Mala nostra pelle,	destroy our wickedness,
	Bona cuncta posce.	pray for all that is good.
4.	Monstra te esse matrem,	Be thou a mother to us;
	Sumat per te preces,	let Him, who deigned for our sake
	Qui pro nobis natus,	to be born your son,
	Tulit esse tuus.	hear our prayers through thine.

Verse	Latin text	English text
5.	Virgo singularis,	Most excellent
	Inter omnes mitis,	and submissive of virgins,
	Nos culpis solutos,	free us from sin,
	Mites fac, et castos.	make us meek and spotless.
6.	Vitam præsta puram,	Grant us a sinless life,
	Iter para tutum:	prepare a safe journey for us
	Ut videntes Iesum,	so that, at the sight of Jesus,
	Semper collætemur.	we may rejoice eternally.
7.	Sit laus Deo Patri,	Praise be to God the Father,
	Summo Christo decus,	glory to Christ the Lord
	Spiritui sancto,	and to the Holy Spirit,
	Tribus[9] honor unus.	the same honour to all three.
	Amen.	Amen.

Note: [9] 'Trinus' in Monteverdi 1610.

Magnificat (Luke 1 : 46-53). Tone 1.

Ma - gni - ficat *   anima   me - a   <u>do</u> -   mi - num.____

Et ex - sultavit spi - ri - tus <u>me</u> -   us: * in Deo salu - <u>ta</u> - <u>ri</u>   <u>me</u> -   -   -   o.____

Verse	Latin text	English text	Part(s) bearing cantus firmus in Magnificat à 6vv	Part(s) bearing cantus firmus in Magnificat à 7vv + 6 insts
1.	Magnificat * anima mea dominum.	My soul doth magnify the Lord.	C then S	C, S part 1
2.	Et exsultavit spiritus meus: * in Deo salutari meo.	And my spirit hath rejoiced * in God my Saviour.	A	A
3.	Quia respexit humilitatem ancillae suae: * ecce enim ex hoc beatam me dicent omnes generationes.	For He hath regarded the lowliness of His handmaid: * for behold from henceforth all generations shall call me blessed.	T	Q
4.	Quia fecit mihi magna qui potens est: * et sanctum nomen eius.	For He that is mighty hath done great things to me: * and holy is His name.	C T	A
5.	Et misericordia eius a progenie in progenies: * timentibus eum.	And His mercy is from generation unto generations * unto them that fear Him.	T	T C
6.	Fecit potentiam in brachio suo: * dispersit superbos mente cordis sui.	He hath showed strength with His arm: * He hath scattered the proud in the imagination of their heart.	A	A
7.	Deposuit potentes de sede: * et exaltavit humiles.	He hath put down the mighty from their seat, * and hath exalted the humble.	T	Q
8.	Esurientes implevit bonis: * et divites dimisit inanes.	He hath filled the hungry with good things: * and the rich He hath sent empty away.	A	C
9.	Suscepit Israel puerum suum: * recordatus misericordiae suae.	He hath received Israel His servant, * being mindful of His mercy.	S C	T
10.	Sicut locutus est ad patres nostros: * Abraham, et semini eius in secula.	As He spake to our forefathers, * Abraham and to his seed for ever.	A	A

Verse	Latin text	English text	Part(s) bearing cantus firmus in Magnificat à 6vv	Part(s) bearing cantus firmus in Magnificat à 7vv + 6 insts
11.	Gloria Patri, et Filio: * et spiritui sancto.	Glory be to the Father, and to the Son, * and to the Holy Ghost.	Q	C
12.	Sicut erat in principio, et nunc, et semper: * et in secula seculorum. Amen.	As it was in the beginning, is now, and ever shall be, * world without end. Amen.	C S	C S (shadowed in A)

Notes

1 Introduction

1 According to Jeffrey Kurtzman (*Essays*, 126–7) three other composers anticipated Monteverdi by publishing collections for Marian Vespers – Francesco Terriera in 1601, Serafino Patta and Giovanni Righi in 1606; in none of them are the motets that they contain interspersed among the psalms.

2 *Sanctissimae Virgini Missa Senis Vocibus ac Vesperae (Venezia: Ricciardo Amadino, 1610)*, facsimile edn, with introduction by Greta Haenen (Peer [Belgium]: Alamire, 1992).

3 Monteverdi, *Vespro della Beata Vergine*, ed. Jerome Roche (London &c.: Eulenburg, 1994) (Edition Eulenburg No. 8024).

4 Monteverdi, *Vespers (1610)*, ed. Clifford Bartlett, revised edn, Autumn 1990 (King's Music, Redcroft, Banks End, Wyton, Huntingdon, Cambridgeshire PE17 2AA, England).

5 Claudio Monteverdi, *Vespers for Soloists, Double Choir, Organ and Orchestra*, ed. Denis Stevens (London: Novello, 1994) (Novello Edition NOV 07 0211).

6 'More Monteverdi Vespers', 637.

2 The 1610 settings and the liturgy of Vespers

1 For a more substantial introduction to the liturgy of the Catholic Church, see Harper, *The Forms*.

2 As, for example, on Andrew Parrott's 1984 recording.

3 The differences between the numbering of the psalms in the Vulgate Bible (and Psalter) and the Authorised Version of the Bible (and the Psalter in the Book of Common Prayer (henceforth BCP)) result from the Vulgate's following the numbering of the Greek Septuagint, while the English versions follow the numbering of the Hebrew text of the psalms. The translations of the psalms in BCP are not always identical to those of the Authorised Version of the Bible.

4 Harper, *The Forms*, 161.

5 As Jeffrey Kurtzman has pointed out (*Essays*, 124), the actual number of psalms in such all-inclusive collections varies between thirteen and twenty-one. The essay in which he makes this point – 'Some Historical Perspectives on the Monteverdi Vespers' – which was also published independently in *Analecta musicologica* 15 (1975), 29–86, provides a broad and very valuable contextual study of Vespers collections in the sixteenth and early seventeenth centuries.

6 This is the feast represented on the 1984 Parrott recording.

7 On lesser feasts the antiphon was sung complete only after the psalm; only the incipit – its opening words – were sung before the psalm; see Armstrong, 'The *Antiphonae*', 90, citing a Tridentine breviary of 1618.

8 Harper, *The Forms*, 157. Although the Council of Trent established norms in these and other matters a certain variety of practice persisted for some years. The variants of text and style found in two Tridentine breviaries published in 1598 and 1603 (see Appendix

1, pp. 101–2) offer one illustration of this. Even the ranking of feasts does not always appear to follow the model suggested by the above list. The *Breviarium Romanum* (Venice, 1598) classifies the more important feasts only as 'duplex' and 'semi-duplex'. On the other hand, the *Breviarii S. Barbarae* (Venice, 1583), which represents the local use of the ducal chapel of Santa Barbara at Mantua, already adopts the classification 'duplex maius': its four ranks of important Feasts are 'duplex maius', 'duplex', 'semi maius' and 'semi'. In the calendar of the 1598 Roman breviary the Feast of the Assumption is ranked as 'duplex': in the Santa Barbara breviary it is 'duplex maius'.

9 In reconstructing a liturgical context for a performance of Monteverdi's Vespers, the *LU* model obviously needs to be modified by reference to texts and music found in late sixteenth- or early seventeenth-century Italian liturgical sources.

10 The conventions used in Ex. 1(b) are those of *LU*, except that underlining is used in place of bold print as being easier to read. In providing pitches for the extra syllables following the accent, I have followed the convention used by Monteverdi, which is not the same as that suggested in *LU* (p. 152). Occasionally, cadential formulae cover two accents: an example can be seen in the tone for 'Lauda Ierusalem' given below in Appendix 2, p. 114. The cadential accents of the psalm tones as shown in *LU* and reproduced in Appendix 2 do not always fall on stressed syllables of the Latin text, as may be seen at the end of verses 6 and 8 of 'Laetatus sum' and more generally in 'Lauda Ierusalem'. In this psalm Monteverdi achieves a much more natural accentuation of the Latin than *LU* by suppressing the final ligature of the psalm tone. This may reflect either a compositional decision or a practice with which he was familiar.

11 The intervals of Modes 7 and 8 can be represented as a scale from G to G on the white notes of the piano. Chants in the two modes differ in their range (ambitus), with Mode 7 chants ranging approximately an octave above the final, but little below it and having D as tenor, while Mode 8 chants range up to about a fifth above and a fourth below the final and have C as tenor; see the Table of modes in Willi Apel, *Gregorian Chant* (Bloomington, IN, 1958), 133, or Donald Jay Grout and Claude V. Palisca, *A History of Western Music*, 5th edn (New York and London, 1996), 55.

12 Harper, *The Forms*, 78.

13 *The Falsobordone*, 67.

14 The treatise seems to have been written by 1585, though it was not printed until 1618; see Bradshaw, *The Falsobordone*, 48, n. 17. The version of Psalm Tone 6 used by Rossi is not the one employed by Monteverdi as the basis of his setting of 'Nisi Dominus', but the first version shown in *LU*, 116; its median cadence encompasses two accents rather than one.

15 Bradshaw, *The Falsobordone*, 46.

16 Viadana was choirmaster of Mantua Cathedral from at least January 1594 probably until 1597.

17 *Cento concerti ecclesiastici opera duodecima 1602, parte prima: concerti a una voce con l'organo*, ed. Claudio Gallico, Monumenti musicali mantovani, 1 (Kassel &c., 1964), 45. The text underlaid in Viadana's print – 'Donec ponam' – is the beginning of the second verse of 'Dixit Dominus', implying that the first verse was sung in plainsong (as in Ex. 2). The remainder of verse 2 has been added editorially.

18 Barblan, *Conservatorio*, 165–7 and 167–71 respectively.

19 In *Monteverdi* and 'Liturgical Problems' respectively.

20 See Redlich, 'Claudio Monteverdi: Some Problems', and Biella, 'La "Messa"'. The case against including the sacred concertos in performances of the 1610 Vespers was argued most forcibly by Denis Stevens: see 'Where are the Vespers of Yesteryear?', 'Monteverdi's Vespers Verified' and the preface to his edition of the Vespers published in 1961, which did not include the concertos. The revised version of this edition (1994) does include them.

21 'Liturgical Problems', 100.

22 *Ibid.*, 98–9 (Banchieri's treatise was first published at Venice in 1605; the 'Table' appears in the revised second edition (Venice, 1611), 45) and 99–100.

23 See Chapter 3, p. 34, for further discussion of the inclusion of 'Duo Seraphim' in the 1610 print.

24 Armstrong, 'The *Antiphonae*'; Moore, *Vespers at St. Mark's*, particularly 175–9; Hucke, 'Die fälschlich so genannte "Marien"-Vesper'.

25 This is the solution adopted, for example, on the 1984 Parrott recording.

26 *Vespers at St. Mark's*, 178.

27 *Caeremoniale Episcoporum* (1600), 152. This injunction remained in force in later printings of the *Caeremoniale*.

28 Moore, *Vespers at St. Mark's*, I. 151–2 and Document 124.

29 Letter of 11 October 1647 to Friedrich Behaim at Nuremberg. Translation by Denis Stevens, 'Monteverdiana 1993', 571–2.

30 Trans. Stevens, 'Monteverdiana 1993', 572–3. Giovanni Rovetta was Monteverdi's assistant and, from 1644, his successor as choirmaster of St Mark's, Venice.

31 Armstrong, 'The *Antiphonae*', 108–10. Interestingly, of the three collections of Marian Vespers published before Monteverdi's, only Patta's (1606) includes five motets; those of Terriera (1601) and Righi (1606) include only four (see Kurtzman, *Essays*, 127).

32 'Blazey, 'A Liturgical Role'; Parrott, 'Getting it Right', 534.

33 See Meier, *The Modes*. Pontio's comments on modal usage are referred to in the analyses contained in Chapters 4 and 5, below.

3 The 1610 print and Monteverdi's career

1 There is some disagreement over the date of Casola's letter. Stefano Davari, 'Notizie biografiche del distinto maestro di musica Claudio Monteverdi', *Atti e memorie della R. Accademia Virgiliana di Mantova* 10 (1884–5), 99, n. 3, gives 16 July 1610, while Emil Vogel, 'Claudio Monteverdi', *Vierteljahrsschrift für Musikwissenschaft* 3 (1887), 430, gives 26 July. Most subsequent authors have followed one or other of these dates, though De' Paoli, *Monteverdi*, 250–1 and 356, gives 10 July. Parisi, 'Ducal Patronage', the most recent archival study of the Mantuan court, gives 16 July 1610 as the date of Casola's letter (II, 575, n. 216).

2 Only one complete copy survives: in Bologna, Civico Museo Bibliografico Musicale. Other, incomplete, copies survive as follows: Brescia, Archivio del Duomo, and Lucca, Biblioteca del Seminario Arcivescovile presso la Curia (both lacking the *Bassus generalis*; the Brescia copy has appended to it an organ score of the Mass prepared by Lorenzo Tonelli: see Kurtzman, *Essays*, 9); Rome, Casanatense Library (T), Rome, Archivio Doria Pamphili (A); Wrocław, Biblioteka Uniwersytecka (C, A, T, B, 7); Stockholm, Kungliga Biblioteket (T). Errors in the listing given in *RISM: Einzeldrucke vor 1800 [RISM]* (Kassel, 1976), II, 53–4, are corrected in Kurtzman, *Essays*, 40, n. 1. Although the collection as a whole was never reprinted, the first two items were reissued, with some variants (see the notes to the edition by Clifford Bartlett), in *Reliquiae sacrorum concentuum Giovan Gabrielis, Iohan-Leonis Hasleri, utriusque praestantissimi musici* (Nuremberg, 1615).

3 See Horsley, 'Full and Short Scores'.

4 The signatures were a guide to the printer when cutting and binding the book. He seems to have saved time by leaving intact as much of the verbal text as possible from one part-book to another, hence the identical title-pages for the seven vocal-instrumental part-books.

5 Slightly adapted from the translation by Roger Bowers, 'Some Reflection', 396.

6 The Latin word 'concentus' is used here in the same sense as the Italian 'concerto', a fashionable term used in the early seventeenth century for motets with instrumental accompaniment, whether continuo only or continuo and melody instruments.

7 Kurtzman, *Essays*, 131, suggests that the ambiguity may have been intended to disguise the uncanonical use of the concertos as antiphon-substitutes.

8 'Where are the Vespers of Yesteryear?' 316–17, and in the preface to his 1961 edition of the Vespers.

9 'The Palace Church', 60.
10 *Essays*, 42, n. 20.
11 Domenico de' Paoli, *Claudio Monteverdi: Lettere, dediche e prefazione* (Rome, 1973), 50, and *idem*, Monteverdi, 253.
12 Parisi, 'Ducal Patronage', 604–5 and notes 408–10. On cardinals Montalto and Borghese respectively, see James Chater, 'Musical Patronage in Rome at the Turn of the Seventeenth Century: the Case of Cardinal Montalto', *Studi musicali* 16 (1987), 179–227, and Jean Lionnet, 'The Borghese Family and Music during the First Half of the Seventeenth Century', *Music & Letters* 74 (1993), 519–29.
13 *Lettere*, ed. Lax, 9–11; *Letters*, trans. Stevens, 71–2.
14 *Essays*, 8–9, 12–13.
15 *Lettere*, ed. Lax, 12; *Letters*, trans. Stevens, 80.
16 For the most thorough-going treatment of Monteverdi's biography see Fabbri, *Monteverdi*.
17 Fabbri, *Monteverdi*, 31. The payroll for the group for August 1595 is given in Fenlon, *Music and Patronage*, I, 194, document 63.
18 Denis Stevens, 'Monteverdiana 1993', speculates that there might have been as many as six singers in the group, but his speculation and the idea that there was a special Vespers service with music by Monteverdi on the eve of the battle of Vysegrad seems to be based on Vincenzo Errante's (1915) gloss on Cardi's account, rather than on the account itself. This latter speculation is repeated in the Preface to the revised version of Professor Stevens's edition of the Vespers.
19 Letter of 28 November 1601 to Duke Vincenzo Gonzaga at Kanizsa (Hungary); *Lettere*, ed. Lax, 13–14; *Letters*, trans. Stevens, 29–30.
20 'The Palace Church', 60.
21 Fenlon, *Music and Patronage*, I, 95–6.
22 On Santa Barbara, see Fenlon, *Music and Patronage*, particularly Chapter 3.
23 Parisi, 'Ducal Patronage', 16.
24 'The Monteverdi Vespers'.
25 The polyphony of the Santa Barbara library is catalogued in Barblan, *Conservatorio*. The two inventories, of 1611 and 1623, discussed by Barblan (pp. xxi–xxv) show that the collection did not include music by Monteverdi even in the seventeenth century. The Santa Barbara plainsong books are located in Mantua, Archivio storico diocesano.
26 'Monteverdi, Kapellmeister'.
27 These are 'Dixit Dominus', 'Confitebor', 'Beatus vir', 'Laudate pueri', 'Laudate Dominum omnes gentes'.
28 *Breviarii S. Barbara*, I, ff. 128ʳ and 181ᵛ respectively.
29 Barblan, *Conservatorio*, 169, 175 and 173 respectively.
30 I understand that a similar conclusion is argued by Paola Besutti in an article forthcoming in the papers of the Monteverdi conference held at Mantua in 1993. I should like to acknowledge with gratitude the help of Mr Gregory Barnett of Princeton University who very kindly transcribed examples of Santa Barbara texts and plainsongs for me.
31 'Monteverdi's Vespers'. See also his article on Amante Franzoni's Mass for St Barbara's Day 1612 – '"Behold our affliction"'. The 1989 recording directed by Harry Christophers is a performance of the 1610 Vespers as a Vespers of St Barbara.
32 *Breviarii S. Barbarae*, I, f. 179ʳ.
33 Barblan, *Conservatorio*, 165–7.
34 See, for example, Kurtzman, *Essays*, 12. This idea also forms the basis of John Eliot Gardiner's hypothesis that the Vespers was specifically written with Venice in mind; see the booklet accompanying his 1990 recording.
35 See Dixon, 'Progressive Tendencies', and Jean Lionnet, 'The Borghese Family and Music during the First Half of the Seventeenth Century', *Music & Letters* 74 (1993), particularly 521–2. The 'secret Vespers' were celebrated in the pope's private apartments on Christmas and Easter days, Pentecost and the feast of St Peter and St Paul. According to Lionnet, the custom of singing these Vespers to organ accompaniment

was established during the reign of Paul V, Monteverdi's dedicatee. On Christmas Day 1616 there were newly composed psalms for three and four choirs and almost all the antiphons were sung in composed settings (see also Lorenzo Bianconi, *Music in the Seventeenth Century*, trans. David Bryant (Cambridge, 1987), 107). Although none of these occasions warranted a Marian Vespers, it would still have been possible to use those settings of Monteverdi's that were common to all celebrations of Vespers.

36 See Palisca, 'The Artusi–Monteverdi Controversy', and Fabbri, *Monteverdi*, 34–52.

37 *Seconda parte dell'Artusi overo Delle imperfettioni della moderna musica* (Venice, 1603).

38 Fabbri, *Monteverdi*, 101–2.

39 Letter of 2 December 1608; *Lettere*, ed. Lax, 20–4, *Letters*, trans. Stevens, 50–4.

40 The inclusion at the end of the volume of a second setting of the Magnificat for voices and organ without concertato instruments does not really upset this view.

41 The letter in which Francesco Gonzaga communicated to his brother his decision to dismiss the Monteverdis is transcribed in Susan Parisi, '"Licenza alla Mantovana": Frescobaldi and the Recruitment of Musicians for Mantua, 1612–15', *Frescobaldi Studies*, ed. A. Silbiger (Durham, N.C., 1987), 60–1.

42 See the documents from the archives of St Mark's reproduced in Denis Arnold, *Monteverdi*, 1st edn (London, 1963), 202, which record the payments made to porters for ferrying two organs to San Giorgio and then returning them, and to twenty players for having taken part in the 'prova della messa del nᵒ maestro di Capella'.

43 Contrary to the suggestion made by John Eliot Gardiner (see the booklet accompanying his 1990 recording), though it is, of course, possible that Monteverdi may have performed items from the 1610 Vespers at Venice during his career there as *maestro di cappella*.

44 Fabbri, *Monteverdi*, 124.

4 'Suited to the chapels or chambers of princes'

1 On late Renaissance and early Baroque singing technique, see Enrico Careri, 'Le tecniche vocali del canto italiano d'arte tra il XVI e il XVII secolo', *Nuova rivista musicale italiana* 18 (1984), 359–75; David Galliver, 'Cantare con la gorga: the Coloratura Technique of the Renaissance Singer', *Studies in Music* 7 (1973), 10–18; Robert Greenlee, 'The Articulation Techniques of Florid Singing in the Renaissance', *Journal of Performance Practice* 1 (1983), 1–19; Greenlee, '"Dispositione di voce": Passage to Florid Singing', *Early Music* 15 (1987), 47–55; Oscar Tajettti and Alberto Colzani, 'Aspetti della vocalità secentesca', *Studi sul primo Seicento* (Como, 1983), 223–309; Richard Wistreich, '"La voce è grata assai, ma ...": Monteverdi on Singing', *Early Music*, 12 (1994), 7–19.

2 Our knowledge of the art of ornamentation in the sixteenth and early seventeenth centuries derives from manuals specifically devoted to teaching singers and instrumentalists how to ornament plain written lines, from treatises covering broader issues of composition and performance, and from surviving examples of music with fully written-out ornamentation. A valuable introduction is provided by Howard Mayer Brown, *Embellishing 16th-Century Music*, Early Music Series 1 (London, 1976).

3 Underlying the music of Monteverdi's 1610 publication, which is notated in a late form of mensural notation, is the idea of a normal and consistent tempo, indicated to performers by a regular down and up motion of the hand (the 'tactus'). The relatively rare appearance of time-words like 'allegro' and 'adagio' indicate deviations from this norm. Signatures such as C and 3/2 indicate the number of notes performed during the space of a tactus: the signature C indicates a semibreve tactus, so that each down- and each up-beat indicates the length of a minim; 3/2 following C indicates that three minims now go where two went before: that is, the speed of the minims is faster, so that three are encompassed by the same tactus [o = o.]. The signature ¢ (tactus alla breve), which literally indicated movement twice as fast as C (each down- and up-beat encompassed a semibreve rather than a minim), was in practice used to indicate a minim pulse 'rather

faster' than the minim pulse under ₵ (the so-called 'tactus celerior'). According to Curt Sachs (*Rhythm and Tempo: a Study in Music History* (New York, 1953), 203) the most frequently cited norm for measuring the length of the tactus was to equate it with the regular pulse of a man with quiet respiration, which gives a metronome measurement of between 60 and 80: thus, under ₵, the tempo would be ♩ = M.M. 60–80. In practice, though, the underlying tempo, though regular for each piece, could be varied by a number of factors: the acoustic in which the piece was to be performed, for example, or the technical difficulty of the piece itself, as indicated in the 'Et exultavit' of the seven-part Magnificat. It is interesting that there is no indication that the much more difficult 'Duo Seraphim' should be taken slowly. For a fuller discussion of Monteverdi's notation and its implications, see Bowers, 'Some Reflection', and the ensuing correspondence between Bowers and Kurtzman in *Music & Letters* 74 (1993), 487–95, and 75 (1994), 145–54. The proportional relationships suggested by Bowers's article are given in the textual notes rather than on the scores of the Roche and Bartlett editions, reflecting the still-contentious nature of this issue.

4 Such ornamentation was to be performed without introducing consonants to aid the articulation and without unduly separating the notes as sometimes happened in Monteverdi performances earlier this century.

5 'Discorso sopra la musica de' suoi tempi' (*c.* 1628); the translation is slightly modified from that given by Carol MacClintock in *Readings in the History of Music in Performance* (Bloomington, 1979), 28–9.

6 Ed. H. Wiley Hitchcock, Recent Researches in the Music of the Baroque Era 9 (Madison, 1970). The *Madrigali per cantare e sonare a uno, due e tre soprani* (Rome, 1601) of Luzzasco Luzzaschi, who was court organist at Ferrara from 1571 to 1597, provides written-out examples of ornamented madrigals sung by the ladies of Ferrara (modern edition, ed. Adriano Cavicchi, Monumenti di musica italiana, serie ii: 'Polifonia', ii (Brescia and Kassel, 1965)).

7 This distinction was drawn by Nicola Vicentino (*L'antica musica ridotta alla moderna prattica* (Rome, 1555), libro IV, Gioseffo Zarlino (*Le istituzioni armoniche* (Venice, 1558), parte terza, caXLVI, f. 253) and Ludovico Zacconi (*Prattica di musica* (Venice, 1592), libro primo, caLX, f. 52ᵛ).

8 *Lettere*, ed. Lax, 49; *Letters*, trans. Stevens, 110.

9 *Le Fêtes du mariage de Ferdinand de Médicis et de Christine de Lorraine, I: Musique des intermèdes de 'La Pellegrina'*, ed. D. P. Walker, Federico Ghisi and Jean Jacquot (Paris, 1963), 3.

10 Bovicelli, *Regole, passaggi di musica, madrigali e motetti passaggiati* (Venice, 1594), 18; Conforto, *Breve e facile maniera d'essercitarsi ad ogni scolaro ... a far passaggi* (Rome, 1593), 22.

11 S. J. Van Dijk and J. Hazelden Walker, *The Origins of the Modern Roman Liturgy* (Westminster, USA, and London, 1960), 232, cited in Hucke, 'Die fälschlich so genannte "Marien"-Vesper', 295 and 303.

12 *Breviarium Romanum, ex decreto Sacrosancti Concilij Tridentini restitutum* (Venice, 1599), f. 193ʳ (*GB–Bu*).

13 Biblical texts are taken from *Biblia Sacra Vulgatae Editionis Sixti Quinti iussu recognita et auctoritate Clementis Octavi edita* (Rome, 1592) (*GB-Lbl*, C.110.k.4).

14 Meier, *The Modes*, 89.

15 Bernhard Meier ('Zur Tonart', 365) has suggested that Monteverdi's choice of Mode 2 for a piece entitled 'Duo Seraphim' is yet another reflection of the opening of the text.

16 Pontio, *Ragionamento*, 99ff., summarised in Meier, *The Modes*, 109. I have chosen to refer to Pontio's definitions alone partly because of his geographical and chronological proximity to the young Monteverdi, partly because, as Meier points out (108), he is an author who 'places more importance on "prattica" and the judgment of the ear than on mathematical erudition' in his observations on modal usage.

17 See Athalya Brenner, *The Song of Songs* (Sheffield, 1989), 55.

18 Pontio admits cadences on C – the mediation of Psalm Tone 8 – as a principal cadence

in Mode 8 'remarking that the attentive composer uses [them] … so that one can better distinguish Mode 8 from Mode 7' (Meier, *The Modes*, 109). In Mode 7, cadences on C are only to be used 'in passing' and with care.

19 *Le nuove musiche*, ed. Hitchcock, 51–2.
20 Not for alto and tenor in dialogue, as suggested in the revised Stevens edition.
21 John Rosselli, 'The Castrati as a Professional Group and a Social Phenomenon, 1550–1850', *Acta musicologica* 60 (1988), 148.
22 Meier, *The Modes*, 244–5.
23 Kurtzman (*Essays*, 20–21) takes a different view of the age of 'Audi cœlum'. He attributes the number of errors found in the original print of 'Audi cœlum' to the printer's having worked from a recently completed, and slipshod, manuscript.
24 The second and third stanzas are, however, based on a verse from the Song of Songs (6:10 in the translation given in the Authorised Version of the Bible).
25 F. W. Sternfeld, 'Aspects of Echo Music in the Renaissance', *Studi musicali* 9 (1980), 45–57.
26 Meier, *The Modes*, 109.
27 Jerome, *Commentarii in Ezechielem*, lib. 13, cap (s.s.) 44, linea 1197. I am very grateful to David Parker and Valerie Edden for help in identifying this reference.
28 John Eliot Gardiner's suggestion of a secondary image here – that of Venice as the gateway to the East – though intriguing, is convincing only if we assume, as he does, that Monteverdi was aiming his collection of Vespers music chiefly at Venice, rather than Rome.
29 Arnold, 'Notes', 60–3.
30 *Essays*, 151–2.
31 'A Liturgical Role', 175.

5 'And all on a *cantus firmus*'

1 Meier, *The Modes*, 241.
2 *Ibid.*, 109; all similar references to cadence centres are based on Pontio's definitions.
3 Meier, *The Modes*, 140.
4 Denis Stevens has speculated ('Monteverdiana 1993', 566–7, and in the preface to his revised (1994) edition of the Vespers) that these rhythms might derive from Monteverdi's encounter with gypsy music while in Hungary. Equally, though, they may be no more than an imaginative extension of an ornamental figure suggested by Caccini in the preface to *Le nuove musiche*.
5 Meier, *The Modes*, 408.
6 For his setting 'Piangono al pianger mio' in *Il primo libro di musiche da cantar solo* (Milan, 1609).
7 Pontio, *Ragionamento*, 113.
8 For a Mantuan example, see the excerpt from Gastoldi's 'Nisi Dominus' printed in Kurtzman, *Essays*, 134–5. On Roman polychoral music, see Dixon, 'Progressive Tendencies', 116–19. On polychoral music in general, see Anthony F. Carver, *Cori spezzati*, 2 vols. (Cambridge, 1988).
9 See Bryant, 'The cori spezzati'.
10 On Monteverdi's registrations, see Luigi Ferdinando Tagliavini, 'Registrazioni organistiche nei Magnificat dei Vespri monteverdiani', *Rivista italiana di musicologia* 2 (1967), 365–71, and Gianfranco Spinelli, 'Confronto fra le registrazioni organistiche dei Vespri di Monteverdi e quelle de "L'arte organica" di Antegnati', *Congresso internazionale sul tema Claudio Monteverdi*, ed. Raffaello Monterosso (Verona, 1969), 479–88.
11 Bowers, 'Some Reflection', 389–91.
12 *Essays*, 71–86.
13 Kurtzman, *Essays*, 86; Bowers, 'Some Reflection', 378–9.
14 *Essays*, 10, 19–20.

15 This conclusion largely agrees with that suggested by Graham Dixon, 'Monteverdi's Vespers', 386.

6 Issues of performance

1 *Johannes Gabrieli*, III, 112–15, and II, 52–8 respectively.
2 *L'arte musicale in Italia*, IV, 51–72.
3 See Redlich, 'Monteverdi's Religious Music', 209, and Redlich, *Claudio Monteverdi*, 154 and 182, n. 27.
4 The dates and places of these performances are listed in the sources cited in note 3. Redlich gives conflicting dates for the performances on Radio Beromünster: '1942–45' in *Claudio Monteverdi* and '1943 and later' in 'Monteverdi's Religious Music'.
5 Michael Tippett, *Those Twentieth-Century Blues: an Autobiography* (London; 1991), 158. Tippett misremembered that the prelude ends on an A major, rather than a D major chord, and also that the edition used was that of Redlich, rather than Goehr. The choir can only have needed to be given the note because the priest's 'Deus in adjutorium' was omitted.
6 *Claudio Monteverdi*, 153 and 128 respectively.
7 *The Times*, 15 May 1946, 6.
8 A 'complete' recording of the Vespers should include only one of the Magnificat settings, though a few listed in the Discography, below, also include the Magnificat à 6 as a supplement.
9 Review of recording of Monteverdi *Vespro*, 138–40.
10 'Correspondence: Editions', 'Correspondence: Monteverdi' (in response to a rather misconceived attack by Schrade demonstrating Redlich's reliance on Malipiero, published in *The Music Review* 14 (1953), 336–40), 'The Editing', 'Some Problems', 'Monteverdi and Schütz', Redlich and Stevens, 'Monteverdi's Vespers'.
11 'Where are the Vespers of Yesteryear?'
12 'Monteverdi's "Vespers" Verified'.
13 This part of the preface is omitted in the revised (1994) version of Stevens's edition, which includes the concertos.
14 'Liturgical Problems'.
15 Vienna & London: Universal (Philharmonia) Edition.
16 'More Monteverdi Vespers', 638.
17 Graham Dixon, 'The Performance of Palestrina: Some Questions, but Fewer Answers', *Early Music* 22 (1994), 671.
18 I am grateful to Laura Davey for information on this subject.
19 See, for example, the discussion in Holman, '"Col nobilissimo esercitio"', particularly 584–5.
20 See Kurtzman, *Essays*, 28, Dixon, 'Continuo Scoring', and, for example, the description of a Vespers directed by Monteverdi at Venice on 24 June 1620, published in Frits Noske, 'An Unknown Work by Monteverdi: the Vespers of St. John the Baptist', *Music & Letters* 66 (1985), 118–22, which was accompanied by 'four theorbos, two cornetts, two bassoons, two violins, a bass viol of monstrous dimensions, organ, and other instruments'. The location of this performance was probably the church of SS Giovanni e Paolo, Venice, not S Giovanni in Bragora as suggested by Noske, and the occasion the annual celebration of St John the Baptist's day funded by the Florentine community at Venice, whose patron saint he was.
21 He uses the combination several times in *Orfeo*; see also his letter of 22 January 1611.
22 Dixon, 'Continuo Scoring'.
23 *Essays*, 37–40.
24 Parrott, 'Transposition'; Kurtzman, 'An Aberration Amplified'. See also Patrizio Barbieri, '*Chiavette* and Modal Transposition in Italian Practice (c. 1500–1837)', *Recercare* 3 (1991), 5–75. More recently, Kurtzman has explored possible origins of the high-clef

convention in 'Tones, Modes, Clefs and Pitch in Roman Cyclic Magnificats of the 16th Century', *Early Music* 22 (1994), 641–4.

25 'Getting it Right'.

26 'Some Reflection'.

27 See their correspondence in *Music & Letters* 74 (1993), 487–95, and 75 (1994), 145–54.

28 The 1995/96 recording under Junghänel acknowledges Bowers's conclusions by adopting a broader triple metre, but produces unconvincing results. The problem here may be that because Junghänel's duple-metre tempi are themselves rather stately, use of the proportions suggested by Bowers produces uncomfortably slow triple passages.

29 Fallows, 'Monteverdi: Vespers (1610)', 1.

Select bibliography

For editions, see Chapters 1 and 6 and the list of Abbreviations

Liturgical sources

Antiphonale Monasticum pro Diurnis Horis juxta vota RR. DD. Abbatum Congregationum Confederatum Ordinis Sancti Benedicti a Solesmensibus Monachis restitutum (Paris, 1934)

Antiphonale Sacrosanctae Romanae Ecclesiae pro Diurnis Horis SS. D. N. Pii X Pontificis Maximi jussu Restitutum et Editum (Rome, 1912). (*GB-Lbl*, 2202. bb.10) (The full title-page is preceded by a shorter one, which reads *Liber Antiphonarium pro Diurnis Horis*)

Breviarii S. Barbarae Gregorii XIII. Pont. Max. Auctoritate approbati. Pars prima. [Secunda.] (Venice, 1583) (*GB-Lbl*, C.36.f.23)

Breviarium Romanum ex decreto Sacrosancti Concilij Tridentini restitutum (Venice, 1598) (*GB-Lbl*, Legg 221)

Breviarium Romanum ex decreto Sacrosancto Concilij Tridentini restitutum (Venice, 1603) (*GB-Lbl*, 843.a.4)

Caeremoniale Episcoporum iussu Clementis VIII. Pont. Max. Novissime reformatum. Omnibus Ecclesijs, praecipue autem Metropolitanis Cathedralibus & Collegiatis perutile ac necessarium (Rome, 1600) (*GB-Bu*, Shakespeare Institute, r16.R6)

Guidetti, Giovanni, *Directorium Chori ad usum omnium Ecclesiarum, Cathedralium, & Collegiatum*, revised Giovanni Francesco Massano (Rome, 1604) (*GB-Lbl*, Legg 25)

Lefebvre, Dom Gaspar, *Saint Andrew Daily Missal, with Vespers for Sundays and Feasts* (Bruges, 1954)

The Liber Usualis, with Introduction and Rubrics in English, edited by the Benedictines of Solesmes (Tournai, 1953)

Psalterium Chorale, una cum Hymnario toto: Secundum morem & consuetudinem Sacrosancte Ecclesie Romane: Dispositum per hebdomadam iuxta ordinem novi Breviarij et decreto Sacrosancti Concilij Tridentum restituti (Venice, 1585) (*GB-Lbl*, C.52.k.1)

Literature

Armstrong, James, 'The *Antiphonae, Seu Sacrae Cantiones* (1613) of Giovanni

Francesco Anerio: a Liturgical Study', *Analecta musicologica* 14 (1974), 89–150

Arnold, Denis, *Monteverdi: Church Music* (London, 1982)

'Monteverdi's Church Music: some Venetian Traits', *Monthly Musical Record* 88 (1958), 83–91

'More Monteverdi Vespers', *Musical Times* 108 (1967), 637–8

Monteverdi, rev. Tim Carter (London, 1990 [1991])

'The Monteverdi Vespers: a Postscript', *Musical Times* 104 (1963), 24–5

'Notes on Two Movements of the Monteverdi Vespers', *Monthly Musical Record* 84 (1954), 59–66

Barblan, Guglielmo, *Conservatorio di Musica 'Giuseppe Verdi' – Milano: Catalogo della biblioteca, fondi speciali, i: Musiche della Cappella di S. Barbara in Mantova* (Florence, 1972)

Biella, Giuseppe, 'La "Messa", il "Vespro" e i "Sacri Concenti" di Claudio Monteverdi nella stampa Amadino dell'anno 1610', *Musica sacra*, serie seconda 9 (1964), 104–15

Blazey, David, 'A Liturgical Role for Monteverdi's *Sonata sopra Sancta Maria*', *Early Music* 17 (1989), 175–82

Bonta, Stephen, 'Liturgical Problems in Monteverdi's Marian Vespers', *Journal of the American Musicological Society* 20 (1967), 87–106

Bowers, Roger, 'Some Reflection upon Notation and Proportions in Monteverdi's Mass and Vespers of 1610', *Music & Letters* 73 (1992), 347–98

Bradshaw, Murray C., *The Falsobordone: a Study in Renaissance and Baroque Music*, Musicological Studies and Documents 24 (Neuhausen-Stuttgart, 1978)

Bryant, David, 'The cori spezzati of St. Mark's: Myth and Reality', *Early Music History* 1 (1981), 165–86

Carter, Tim, *Music in Late Renaissance and Early Baroque Italy* (London, 1992)

De' Paoli, Domenico, *Monteverdi* (Milan, 1945; enlarged second edn, Milan, 1979)

Dixon, Graham, '"Behold our Affliction": Celebration and Supplication in the Gonzaga Household', *Early Music* 24 (1996), 251–61

'Continuo Scoring in the Early Baroque: the Role of Bowed-Bass Instruments', *Chelys* 15 (1986), 38–53

'Monteverdi's Vespers of 1610: "della Beata Vergine"?', *Early Music* 15 (1987), 386–9

'Progressive Tendencies in the Roman Motet during the Early Seventeenth Century', *Acta musicologica* 53 (1981), 105–19

Fabbri, Paolo, *Monteverdi*, trans. Tim Carter (Cambridge, 1994)

Fallows, David, 'Monteverdi: Vespers (1610)', *Choral Music on Record*, ed. Alan Blyth (Cambridge, 1991), 1–9

Fenlon, Iain, *Music and Patronage in Sixteenth-Century Mantua* (Cambridge, 1980, 1982)

'The Monteverdi Vespers: Suggested Answers to Some Fundamental Questions', *Early Music* 5 (1977), 380–7

Select bibliography

Harper, John, *The Forms and Orders of Western Liturgy from the Tenth to the Eighteenth Century: a Historical Introduction and Guide for Students and Musicians* (Oxford, 1991)

Holman, Peter, '"Col nobilissimo esercitio della vivuola": Monteverdi's String Writing', *Early Music* 21 (1993), 577–90

Holschneider, Andreas, 'Zur Aufführungspraxis der Marien-Vesper von Monteverdi', *Hamburger Jahrbuch für Musikwissenschaft* 1 (1974), 59–68

Horsley, Imogene, 'Full and Short Scores in the Accompaniment of Italian Church Music in the Early Baroque', *Journal of the American Musicological Society* 30 (1977), 466–99

Hucke, Helmut, 'Die fälschlich so gennante "Marien"-Vesper von Claudio Monteverdi', *Bericht über den Internationalen Musikwissenschaftlichen Kongress Bayreuth, 1981*, ed. Christoph-Hellmut Mahling and Siegrid Wiesmann (Kassel, 1984), 295–305

Jeppesen, Knud, 'Monteverdi, Kapellmeister an S.ta Barbara?' *Congresso internazionale sul tema Claudio Monteverdi e il suo tempo*, ed. R. Monterosso (Verona, 1969), 313–19

Kurtzman, Jeffrey G., *Essays on the Monteverdi Mass and Vespers of 1610*, Rice University Studies 64/4 (Houston, 1978)

'An Abberation Amplified', *Early Music* 13 (1985), 73–6

Leopold, Silke, *Monteverdi: Music in Transition*, trans. Anne Smith (Oxford, 1991)

Meier, Bernhard, 'Zur Tonart der Concertato-Motetten in Monteverdis "Marienvesper"', *Claudio Monteverdi: Festschrift Reinhold Hammerstein zum 70. Geburtstag*, ed. Ludwig Finscher (Laaber, 1986), 359–67

The Modes of Classical Vocal Polyphony, trans. Ellen S. Beebe (New York, 1988)

Monteverdi, Claudio, *Claudio Monteverdi: Lettere*, ed. Éva Lax, Studi e testi per la storia della musica 10 (Florence, 1994)

The Letters of Claudio Monteverdi, trans. and introduced Denis Stevens (rev. edn, Oxford, 1995)

Moore, James H., *Vespers at St. Mark's: Music of Alessandro Grandi, Giovanni Rovetta and Francesco Cavalli*, 2 vols. (Ann Arbor, 1981)

Osthoff, Wolfgang, 'Unità liturgica e artistica nei Vespri del 1610', *Rivista italiana di musicologia* 2 (1967), 314–27

Palisca, Claude V., 'The Artusi–Monteverdi Controversy', *The New Monteverdi Companion*, ed. Denis Arnold and Nigel Fortune (London, 1985), 127–58

Parisi, Susan, 'Ducal Patronage of Music in Mantua, 1587–1627: an Archival Study', Ph.D. thesis, University of Illinois at Urbana-Champaign (1989)

Parrott, Andrew, 'Getting it Right', *Musical Times* 136 (1995), 531–5

'Transposition in Monteverdi's Vespers of 1610', *Early Music* 12 (1984), 490–516

Pontio, Pietro, *Ragionamento di Musica* (Parma, 1588), facsimile edn, ed. Suzanne Clercx, Documenta Musicologica, Erste Reihe, 16 (Kassel &c.: Bärenreiter, 1959)

Prunières, Henri, *La vie et l'œuvre de C. Monteverdi* (Paris, 1926); Eng. trans. Marie D. Mackie (London, 1926)

Redlich, Hans F., 'Claudio Monteverdis Kirchenmusik', *Anbruch* 17 (1935), 42–4

    'Correspondence: Editions of Monteverdi's Vespers of 1610', *The Gramophone* 31 (1954), 503

    'Correspondence: Monteverdi', *The Music Review* 15 (1954), 87–8

    'Monteverdi and Schütz in New Editions', *The Music Review* 19 (1958), 72–4

    'Monteverdi's Religious Music', *Music & Letters* 27 (1946), 208–15

    'The Editing of Monteverdi', *Renaissance News* 7 (1954), 50–2

    Claudio Monteverdi: Life and Works, trans. Kathleen Dale (London, 1952); revised version of *Claudio Monteverdi: Leben und Werk* (Olten, 1949)

    'Claudio Monteverdi: Some Problems of Textual Interpretation', *The Musical Quarterly* 41 (1955), 66–75

Redlich, Hans F. and Denis Stevens, 'Letters to the Editor: Monteverdi's Vespers', *Musical Times* 102 (1961), 564–5

Roche, Jerome, 'Monteverdi and the Prima Prattica', *The New Monteverdi Companion*, ed. Denis Arnold and Nigel Fortune (London, 1985), 159–82

Schrade, Leo, *Monteverdi, Creator of Modern Music* (London, 1950/*R*1964)

    Review of recording of Monteverdi, *Vespro della Beata Vergine* (1610), ed. Hans F. Redlich, *The Musical Quarterly* 40 (1954), 138–45

Stevens, Denis, *Monteverdi: Sacred, Secular and Occasional Music* (Cranbury, NJ, 1978)

    'Monteverdi's Vespers Verified', *The Musical Times* 102 (1961), 422

    'Monteverdiana 1993', *Early Music* 22 (1993), 565–74

    'Where are the Vespers of Yesteryear?' *The Musical Quarterly* 3 (1961), 315–30

Tagmann, Pierre, 'The Palace Church of Santa Barbara in Mantua, and Monteverdi's Relationship to its Liturgy', *Festival Essays for Pauline Alderman: a Musicological Tribute*, ed. Burton L. Karson *et al.* (Provo, UT: Brigham Young University Press, 1976), 53–60

Terry, R. R., *Catholic Church Music* (London, 1907)

Winterfeld, Carl von, *Johannes Gabrieli und sein Zeitalter* (Berlin, 1834)

Discography

The following list includes only performances of the 1610 Vespers which claim some degree of completeness (usually such recordings include only the seven-part version of the Magnificat with obbligato instruments, though a few add the six-part setting as a supplement). At the time of writing, no fewer than fourteen 'complete' recordings are available. These are marked with asterisks in the list below and are annotated with regard to the performance solutions adopted (see Chapter 6 for the significance of these). All performances use the pitch standard a' = 440. References to the items included and their ordering use the numbering given below.

1   Domine ad adiuvandum
2   Dixit Dominus
3   Nigra sum
4   Laudate pueri
5   Pulchra es
6   Lætatus sum
7   Duo Seraphim
8   Nisi Dominus
9   Audi cœlum
10 Lauda Ierusalem
11 Sonata sopra Sancta Maria
12 Ave maris stella
13 Magnificat à 7
14 Magnificat à 6

1953   (Redlich edn) (1–13, omitting 8 and 10; performed in order 1, 7, 2, 3, 6, 5, 4, 9, 12, 11, 13) dir. Grischkat. Vox PL 7902
1953   (Schrade edn) (1–13) dir. Lewis. Oiseau Lyre OL 50021–2
1955   (Ghedini edn) (1, 3, 10, 12, 2, 11, 13 and 'O quam pulchra es' (1625)) dir. Stokowski. University of Illinois CRS 1
*1966/67 (1–13, with 11 and 12 reversed) dir. Jürgens. Telefunken AWT/SAWT 9501–2; now Teldec 4509–92175–2. Psalms and Magnificat are prefaced and followed by a series of antiphons chosen, for the most part, on the basis that their modes and endings match those of the psalm tones used by Monteverdi and that their texts are drawn from the Song of Songs (the

exception is the antiphon to the Magnificat 'Sancta Maria, succurre miseris', which is not drawn from the Song of Songs and requires tone 4E instead of 1D). The antiphons do not, therefore, represent a recognised liturgy. First recording to use period instruments. Employs contrasts of choir and soloists and instrumental doubling of voices. 'Lauda Ierusalem' and 'Magnificat' not transposed.

1967 (1–13 in order 1, 2, 9, 8, 5, 6, 12, 11, 4, 7, 10, 3, 1) dir. Craft. (US) Columbia Set M 2 L 2(?3)63

1967 (Stevens edn) (1, 2, 4, 6, 8, 10, 12, 13) dir. Stevens. US Vanguard Cardinal VCS 10001–2: (UK) Vanguard VSL 11000–1

1967/68 (1–13) dir. Le Roux. Concert Hall Society SMS 2518

1967 (1–14) dir. Corboz. Erato STU 70325–7

1968 (1, 2, 4, 6, 8, 10, 12, 13) dir. Biella. Musica Antiqua S PAB 1306/7

1970 (Goehr edn) (1–12) dir. Koch. Eterna 8 26 086/7

*1974 (1–13) dir. Gardiner. Decca 414 572–3; now Decca 443–482 2DF2. Concert performance. Modern instruments except for period continuo group. Employs contrasts of choir and soloists and instrumental doubling of vocal lines. 'Lauda Ierusalem' and Magnificat not transposed.

1975 Dir. Schneidt. Archiv 2723 043. Uses men and boys only. Also includes 1610 Mass.

1976 (1–13) dir. Ledger. EMI ASD 3256/7

1976 Dir. Segarra. Harmonia Mundi HM 1C 165–99681/2. Uses men and boys only.

1983 Dir. Corboz. Erato ECD 88024

1983 Dir. Maruch. Titanic TI 120/1

*1984 (1–13 in order 1–6, 8–10, 12–13, 11, 7, with other items added) dir. Parrott. EMI Reflexe EX 27 0129 3; now EMI CDS 7 47078–8. Complete liturgical reconstruction of Second Vespers for the Feast of the Assumption of the Blessed Virgin (15 August). Choir is used for Nos. 1, 8, 10, 12, 13, else one voice per part. Period instruments. No instrumental doubling of vocal lines except where indicated by Monteverdi in the Magnificat. 'Lauda Ierusalem' and Magnificat transposed down a fourth.

*1987 Dir. Harnoncourt. Teldec 8.35710; now Teldec 4509 92629 2. Semi-liturgical.

*1987 Dir. Herreweghe. Harmonia Mundi HMC 90 1247/8. 'Lauda Ierusalem' and Magnificat transposed down a fourth.

*1989 Issued as *Vespers of Santa Barbara.* (1–13 in order 1–2, 5, 4, 6, 3, 8, 10, 7, 13, 9, 11 adapted to text 'Sancta Barbara, ora pro nobis'; 12 added as supplement; other items added) dir. Christophers. Hyperion CDA 66311/12. Complete liturgical reconstruction of Second Vespers for the Feast of St Barbara (4 December) (Mantua, Santa Barbara rite). Period instruments. Employs contrasts of choir and soloists and some instrumental doubling of vocal lines. 'Lauda Ierusalem' and Magnificat not transposed.

*1989 (1–13, but 11 placed after 13) dir. Bernius. Deutsche Harmonia Mundi

RD 77760. Uses the same sequence of antiphons as Jürgens 1966/67 recording and presumably for the same reason. Also includes the *Capitulum* and versicle and response from the Common of Feasts of the Blessed Virgin, and the Benedicamus Domino, but omits the Collect. Though all this gives the impression of a liturgical reconstruction, it does not represent a recognised liturgy. Period instruments. Employs contrasts of choir and soloists and some instrumental doubling of vocal lines. 'Lauda Ierusalem' and Magnificat not transposed.

*1989   (1–13) dir. Savall. Astrée E 8719. Not a full liturgical performance, but the psalms and Magnificat are prefaced by the antiphons for Second Vespers of the Feast of St Barbara (4 December) from the Santa Barbara, Mantua, rite. Period instruments. Employs contrasts of choir and soloists and instrumental doubling of vocal lines. 'Lauda Ierusalem' transposed down a tone; Magnificat untransposed. Recorded in Santa Barbara, Mantua.

*1990   (1–14) dir. Gardiner. Archiv 429 565–2AH2. Also on video (1–13): Archiv 072.148–3AH. Concert performance. Period instruments. Employs contrasts of choir and soloists and instrumental doubling of vocal lines. 'Lauda Ierusalem' and Magnificats not transposed. Recorded in St Mark's, Venice.

*1991   (1–13, but 11 placed after 13) dir. Pickett. Oiseau-Lyre 425 823–2OHZ. Not a full liturgical reconstruction, but the psalms and Magnificat are prefaced and followed by the antiphons for Second Vespers of the Feast of the Nativity of the Blessed Virgin (8 September). Performed almost entirely with one voice per part. Period instruments. A little instrumental doubling of vocal parts. 'Lauda Ierusalem' and Magnificat transposed down a fourth.

*1995   (Bartlett edn) (1–13) The Scholars, dir. Van Asch. Naxos 8 550662–3. Concert performance. One singer per part. Period instruments. A little instrumental doubling of vocal parts. 'Lauda Ierusalem' transposed down a tone; Magnificat not transposed.

*1995   Dir. Otto. Capr 10 516

*1995/6   (Bartlett edn) (1–13) dir. Junghänel. Deutsche Harmonia Mundi 05472 77332 2. Concert performance. One singer per part. Period instruments. No instrumental doubling of vocal parts except where indicated by Monteverdi. 'Lauda Ierusalem' transposed down a tone; Magnificat not transposed.

*1996   Dir. Jacobs. Soloists, Nederlands Kamerkor, Concerto Vocale. Harmonia Mundi 901566.67.

Index

1610 publication, Monteverdi's (*Missa
    ... ac Vespera*) 1–2, 3–4, 6, 7,
    9, 10, 16, 19, 21, 23–9, 35–40,
    82, 92
  dedicatory letter of 26–7
  early performances of Vespers music,
    theories on 2–3, 23, 30–5, 43
  Mass 'In illo tempore' 1, 24ff., 28,
    35, 38, 39, 83
  organ score in 4, 24–5, 123
  period of composition of 3, 39, 81
  surviving copies of 28, 123
  textual variants in 100–102
  title-pages of 25–6
  Vespers music in (see also 'Editions';
    'Performance practice'; 'Plainsong')
    1–3, 6, 15–16, 23, 24ff., 39, 81,
    82–5
    Audi cœlum 16, 24, 34, 43, 44,
      54–6, 83, 104, 113–14, 127
    Ave maris stella 7, 16, 21, 32,
      33–4, 76–7, 79, 86, 93, 100ff.,
      103, 116–18
    Dixit Dominus 3, 7, 14, 16, 21,
      62–4, 81, 82, 86, 88, 100, 101,
      102, 106–7
    Domine ad adiuvandum 9, 16, 21,
      24, 32, 61–2, 91, 105
    Duo Seraphim 16, 18, 22, 24, 34,
      41, 43–7, 59, 104, 111, 126
    Lætatus sum 3, 7, 16, 24, 44,
      67–72, 79, 81, 100, 101, 102,
      110–11
    Lauda Ierusalem 7, 16, 33, 74–5,
      79, 81, 83, 90–1, 94, 102,
      114–15, 122, 135, 136

Laudate pueri 7, 16, 24, 64–7, 79,
  88, 102, 108–9
Magnificat 1, 2, 4, 6, 7, 8ff.,
  12ff. 14, 16ff., 21, 24, 32, 39, 60,
  77–81, 82ff., 86, 88, 90–1, 92ff.,
  98, 102ff., 118–20, 125, 126,
  128, 134ff.
Nigra sum 4, 16, 24, 43, 47–53,
  54, 104, 107
Nisi Dominus 7, 16, 60–1, 72–4,
  81, 83, 104, 112–13, 122
Pulchra es 9, 16, 24, 47–50, 53–4,
  104, 109
Sonata sopra Sancta Maria 1, 16,
  17–18, 21–2, 34, 39, 44,
  56–9, 82, 84, 86, 87, 93, 116

Anerio, Felice 20–1
Antiphon(s) 8, 9, 10–13, 14, 15–22,
  48, 49, 53, 92, 94, 95–8, 121, 125,
  134–5, 136
  -substitutes 17–22, 47, 85, 123
  seasonal 7, 20
Antiphoner 7, 9
Armstrong, James 18
Arnold, Denis 4–5, 87, 125
Artusi, Giovanni Maria 27, 35–6, 38
Assumption, Feast of the (see 'Liturgy')

Banchieri, Adriano 17, 18, 122
Barnett, Gregory 124
Basile, Adriana 28
Bernius, Frieder 16, 87, 135–6
Besutti, Paola 124
Biella, Giuseppe 122, 135
Blazey, David 21, 56

137